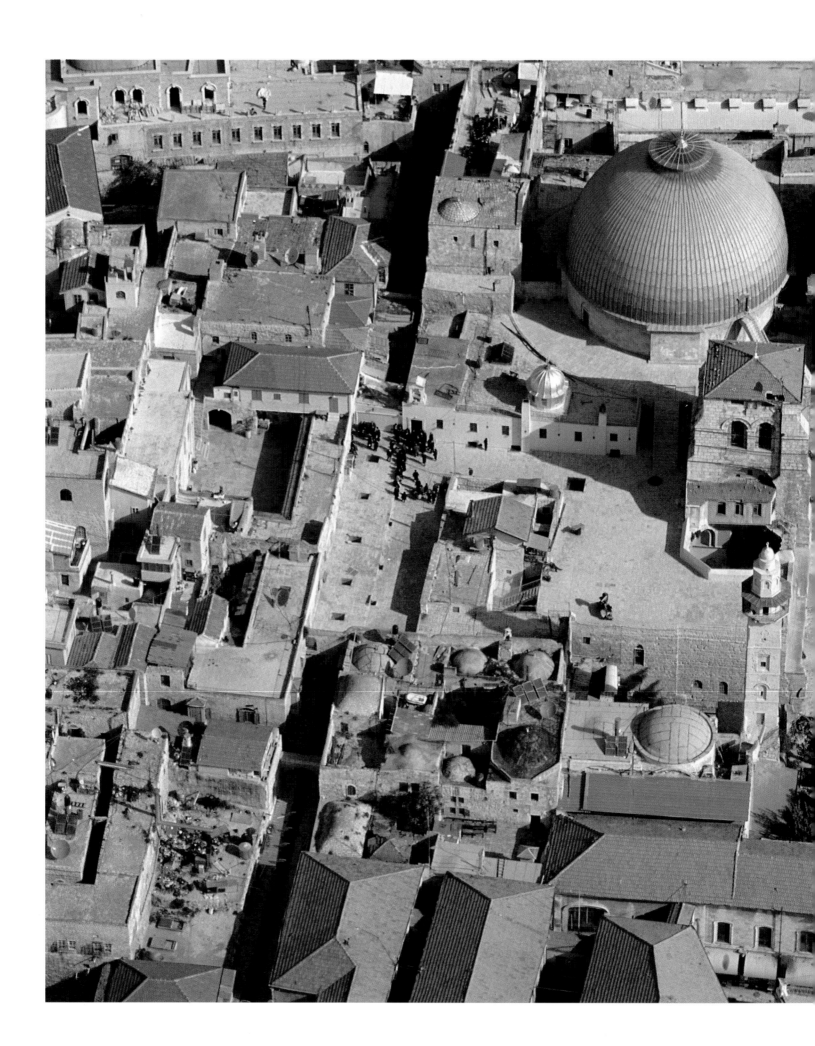

THE CHURCH
OF THE HOLY SEPULCHRE

THE CHURCH OF THE HOLY SEPULCHRE

Text by
Martin Biddle, Gideon Avni,
Jon Seligman, Tamar Winter

Photos by
Michèl Zabé and Garo Nalbandian

RIZZOLI NEW YORK

in cooperation with ISRAEL ANTIQUITIES AUTHORITY

Previous pages:

pp.2-3: The Rotunda of the Church of the Holy Sepulchre. On the right, Easter Mass celebrated by the Latin Patriarch in front of the tomb of Christ and to the left a group of Coptic clergy gathered for their Palm Sunday service.

pp.4-5: An aerial photograph of the Church of the Holy Sepulchre. In the central foreground is the entrance courtyard (Parvis) and above it the two domes of the church.

pp.6-7: Members of the Armenian Brotherhood of St. James kneel in prayer on the Tuesday of Easter.

pp.8-9: The Latin Palm Sunday procession.

pp.10-11: Devotional candles illuminate the exterior of the tomb of Christ.

p.12: Pilgrims await the arrival of the Good Friday procession from the Via Dolorosa.

p.13: The facade of the Edicule resplendent in its elaborate Easter decoration.

First published in the United States of America in 2000
by Rizzoli International Publications, Inc.
300 Park Avenue South, New York, NY 10010

Copyright © 2000 RCS Libri S.p.A., via Mecenate 91, Milano

ISBN 0-8478-2282-6
LC 00-101908

Libri Illustrati Rizzoli
Editor: Luisa Sacchi
Coordinating editor: Cristina Sartori, Barbara Villani
Graphic design and layout:
Sottsass Associati/
Mario Milizia, Paola Lambardi

American Edition:
Jacket layout: Elena Pozzi
Revision: Simona Pagano
Typesetting: Paola Lambardi

Printed and bound in Italy.

Contents

Preface

An anonymous Christian pilgrim who came to Jerusalem from the city of Bordeaux in or around the year A.D. 333 mentioned that a new basilica of the Lord was being built in the center of the holy city. Only seven years had passed since the discovery of the Tomb of Jesus by Makarios, bishop of Jerusalem, who had sought it out under the instructions of Emperor Constantine. Eusebius, the prominent church father of that age, informs us that the tomb was miraculously discovered underneath the Temple of Aphrodite. This was the main temple of Aelia Capitolina, the Roman city that was built on top of the ruins of Jewish Jerusalem. As ordered by Constantine and in part supervised by his mother, Empress Helena, construction soon began on a magnificent shrine to commemorate the holy site. The church was inaugurated in September 335 and became the most venerated Christian sanctuary, a destination for prayer and pilgrimage to this very day.

Numerous compositions by scholars, pilgrims, and other travelers over the past sixteen-and-a-half centuries provide us with detailed descriptions of the sacred compound, its development, and its history. The church has undergone many cycles of destruction and reconstruction. Extensive remodeling under the Crusaders in the twelfth century, for instance, disguised the original spatial arrangement of the architectural complex and bestowed its present shape. Further large-scale construction feats took place in later centuries, each reflecting the needs and tastes of their eras.

The ongoing rebuilding process and the accumulation of chapels on different levels, both within and abutting the church buildings, have enriched the compound of the Holy Sepulchre. At the same time they have made the study of the architectural history of the church complex a daunting task. The available literary descriptions, although of great importance, do not provide a clear picture in the absence of a meticulous survey of the existing remains. An analytical study of this kind began in the late nineteenth century and has continued throughout the twentieth century.

A series of surveys and excavations has accompanied the process of renovation and reshaping of the various parts of the church, a process accelerated during the second half of the twentieth century. The work done by V. Corbo, A. Couasnon, A. Economopoulos, M. Broshi, G. Lavas and numerous other scholars, on behalf of the religious communities who share the Church of the Holy Sepulchre has greatly enriched our understanding of the compound's history. Still, the church is full of secrets. Walls, halls, and hidden spaces are constantly being discovered as restoration proceeds. The authors of this volume, who have dedicated great efforts to the study of various elements within the church, are responsible for some of these recent discoveries.

At the end of the first millennium, the Church of the Holy Sepulchre faced a gloomy future; indeed it suffered an almost total destruction in 1009. At the end of the second millennium, the architectural complex of the Holy Sepulchre is undergoing reconstruction and renovation as it prepares to embrace the multitudes of believers who will visit it during the year 2000.

We all hope and pray that the near future heralds a new age of peace and understanding, and that the numerous pilgrims and visitors to the Church of the Holy Sepulchre will encourage the flowering of tolerance and harmony in Jerusalem, the City of Peace.

Yoram Tsafrir
Professor of Archaeology at the Hebrew University of Jerusalem

A Time Line

A.D. 30/33: A tomb is rock-cut by Joseph of Arimathea and used for the burial of Jesus. The empty tomb probably remained visible until a Roman temple was built over it in A.D. 135.

70: Siege and destruction of Jerusalem by the Romans.

130: The Roman emperor Hadrian founds the colony of Aelia Capitolina on the site of Jerusalem and in A.D. 135 builds a pagan temple over the sites of Golgotha and the tomb.

313: The Roman emperors Constantine and Licinius recognize the legality of the Christian church.

325-326: Makarios, bishop of Jerusalem, acting with Emperor Constantine's approval and guided by the known site of Golgotha, demolishes the pagan temple and discovers under its platform what is identified as the Tomb of Christ. Constantine orders the construction of the Church of the Holy Sepulchre, consisting of the domed Rotunda of the Anastasis (the Resurrection) and the Edicule over the tomb, the Parvis, the court before the cross, and the basilica of the Marturion.

327-328: Empress Helena, mother of Constantine, makes an imperial progress to the eastern provinces including Palestine. She founds the Church of the Nativity in Bethlehem and the Eleona church on the Mount of Olives, and must have inspected and perhaps endowed the construction of the Church of the Holy Sepulchre on her son's behalf. Wood believed to be the remains of the True Cross is found in the course of the work.

420: Emperor Theodosius II erects on Golgotha a richly jeweled golden cross.

614: The Persians capture and sack Jerusalem, and loot the Church of the Holy Sepulchre. The relic of the True Cross is taken to Persia.

630: The Byzantine emperor Heraclius, having invaded Persia and recovered the relic of the True Cross, personally replaces it in the Church of the Holy Sepulchre.

638: Jerusalem surrenders to the Muslims. Caliph 'Umar declines to pray in the Church of the Holy Sepulchre, which remains undisturbed in Christian hands for the next four centuries.

809-829: The dome over the Rotunda of the Anastasis is rebuilt as an open cone, a form it was to keep for a thousand years, until 1809–1810.

870: In this year or shortly before, Bernard the Monk makes the first known record of the ceremony of the Holy Fire on the Saturday of Holy Week.

937: The Church of the Holy Sepulchre is damaged by riots.

966: The church is again damaged by riots.

1009: The Church of the Holy Sepulchre is demolished by order of Caliph al-Hakim, the Fatimid ruler of Egypt, but parts of the tomb and the walls of the Rotunda of the Anastasis survive.

1012-1023: The first stage in the rebuilding of the Church of the Holy Sepulchre.

1027: Great pilgrimages are made to Jerusalem in this and the following years, to celebrate the millennium of Christ's crucifixion and resurrection, and to attend the ceremony of the Holy Fire at the rebuilt Edicule around the tomb.

1037-1041: The Byzantine emperor Michael IV, the Paphlagonian, completes the rebuilding of the Church of the Holy Sepulchre.

1099: The Crusaders capture and sack Jerusalem, and within a few years place a silver figure of Christ on top of the Edicule.

1149: The Crusaders dedicate their reconstruction of the chapels surrounding and enclosing the Rock of Golgotha (Calvary).

1163-1167: The Crusaders complete their reconstruction of the Church of the Holy Sepulchre by building a new choir and transepts, the great south facade, and the bell tower.

1187: Jerusalem surrenders to Saladin. The Latin patriarch and clergy leave the city, but the Church of the Holy Sepulchre remains untouched.

1229: The Crusaders recover Jerusalem by treaty for ten years.

1244: The Khwarizmian Turks capture and sack Jerusalem and loot the Church of the Holy Sepulchre, massacring all those they find there.

1291: The fall of Acre and the final departure of the Crusaders from the Holy Land.

1517: The Ottoman Turks capture Palestine. Sultan Sulayman the Magnificent rebuilds the walls of Jerusalem. The Church of the Holy Sepulchre remains untouched.

1555: The Edicule is rebuilt from its foundations by Boniface of Ragusa, Franciscan Custos of the Holy Land.

1808: The Church of the Holy Sepulchre is badly damaged by fire.

1809-1810: Greek architect Nikolaos Komnenos conducts the restoration of the Church of the Holy Sepulchre.

1852: Sultan 'Adb al-Majid I issues a *firman* (edict) that defines the Status Quo, under which the communities in the Church of the Holy Sepulchre and at other Christian holy places in the Levant have since lived.

1868: Rebuilding of the dome of the Rotunda of the Anastasis.

1917: The British capture Jerusalem and assure all religions that they will remain secure in their buildings and possessions, and that the Status Quo will be maintained.

1927: An earthquake strikes Jerusalem. The Church of the Holy Sepulchre is severely shaken and over the next few years is scaffolded to prevent collapse.

1948: The British leave Jerusalem. After the 1948 Arab-Israeli War, the government of Jordan maintains the Status Quo in the Church of the Holy Sepulchre.

1958: The three "great communities" (Greek Orthodox, Latin [Roman Catholic] and Armenian) establish the Common Technical Bureau to undertake the restoration of the Church of the Holy Sepulchre, which takes place over the next twenty years.

1967: After the 1967 war, the State of Israel maintains the Status Quo in the Church of the Holy Sepulchre.

1997: The newly decorated dome over the Rotunda of the Anastasis is inaugurated, in preparation for the Great Jubilee of the year 2000.

2000: The second millennium of Christ's birth.

The History of the Church of the Holy Sepulchre

Introduction

Jesus was executed outside Jerusalem in 30 or perhaps A.D. 33. Ten years later the places of his crucifixion and burial were incorporated within the walls by the expansion of the city. Decades later these places were buried beneath immense dumps of rubble brought in by the Romans to level the area. Even so, Golgotha, the place of crucifixion, was still a recognized site inside the city three centuries later. It served as a landmark for excavations that uncovered several rock-cut tombs beneath the rubble. One of these tombs was immediately hailed as the Tomb of Christ, though no record of the basis for the choice is known. The emperor Constantine ordered that Golgotha and the tomb should be preserved and embellished, and that a great church should be erected beside them. This basilica, known as the Marturion — "The Testimony" or "The Witness" — was dedicated on 13 September 335 inside the walls of the Roman veteran colony of Aelia Capitolina, soon again to be known by the ancient name of Jerusalem.

For the last seventeen centuries this great complex of buildings, now called the Church of the Holy Sepulchre, or to use its Greek name, the Church of the Anastasis, "the Resurrection," has stood within the walls of Jerusalem. Often damaged, once virtually demolished, but always restored, the church and the holy places within it, Golgotha and above all the tomb, have been throughout these centuries the goal of countless thousands of pilgrims from all over the world. Then, as now, these pilgrims did not find a hill outside a city wall and a tomb in a garden nearby. They found instead a walled city and hidden in the heart of the city, reached by narrow and crowded streets, a vast church that came into view only at the last moment, at the last turn in the street.

These pilgrims traveled to Jerusalem because it contained so many places associated with the life and last days of Jesus, but above all because it contained the Tomb of Christ, the place of his resurrection, the place of their salvation, the Saving, the Life-Giving Tomb. Their first view of Jerusalem, after a long and perilous journey, was a moment of high emotion. Whether coming from the south along the road from Egypt through Bethlehem or from the north from Acre or from Jaffa through Ramla, pilgrims would fall to their knees and weep, as many recorded in accounts of their journeys. For many, Jerusalem came first into sight from the distant hill that is the traditional site of the tomb of the prophet Samuel, Nabi Samwil today. It was from this hill that the Crusaders first saw Jerusalem on the morning of 7 June 1099, and here that they later built the church of Mons Gaudii, Montjoie. From here in 1192 Richard the Lionheart looked down on the city he had come to liberate but was never to enter. Seven centuries

A detail of the exterior of the Edicule.

later a British post on this hill, controlling the road from Jaffa, played a key role in Allenby's capture of Jerusalem on 9 December 1917.

When the pilgrims went home, they took with them from the Church of the Holy Sepulchre remembrances of the Tomb of Christ, oil from the lamps burning above it, strips of cloth or paper showing its exact length, scraps of the rock from Golgotha or from the tomb itself. Others made notes, took careful measurements, and made drawings, even bringing artists with them to do so. They purchased models of the church in stone or wood, or smaller models of Golgotha or the tomb. And after their return some wrote accounts of what they had seen and some built copies of the inside of the tomb, as in the Jeruzalemkerk in Bruges, or in the crypt of the chapel of La Hougue Bie on Jersey. Others erected the whole tomb full-scale, complete with the Edicule, the little house that enclosed it, as at Eichstätt in Bavaria or in the Tuscan hills at San Vivaldo in Valdelsa. And in eastern lands a few even constructed replicas of the whole Church of the Holy Sepulchre, most remarkably at the Novierusalimsky Monastyr, near Istra, east of Moscow. They did these things for remembrance and to provide a setting in which the events of Christ's death and resurrection could be celebrated each year in the Easter liturgy.

These pilgrim words, drawings, models, and actual buildings provide a record, established over a period of more than a thousand years, of what the Church of the Holy Sepulchre has looked like through the centuries and more particularly of the Edicule which surrounds and protects whatever still remains of the rock-cut Tomb of Christ. But the greatest witness is the Church of the Holy Sepulchre itself, its domes and campanile visible from afar rising over the roofs of the Old City.

Jerusalem from the east in medieval times. In the foreground is the El Aqsa mosque and the Dome of the Rock on the Temple Mount. Above the Dome of the Rock, slightly to the right, is the Church of the Holy Sepulchre. In the background, on the line of the city wall, is the citadel of Jerusalem also known as the Tower of David. Jerusalem, the Holy City by F. Hogenberg - G. Braun, copper engraving 1576.

The Crucifixion and Burial of Christ
A.D. 30/33

Detail of a 16th-century silvered bronze altar in the Latin Chapel of the Calvary, depicting the crucifixion. The altar was presented by Ferdinand I de' Medici.

The day before Passover Jesus of Nazareth dined with his twelve disciples. When the Last Supper ended they went out together to the garden of Gethsemane beyond the Kidron Valley, where Jesus was betrayed by Judas and arrested. During the night and early morning of Passover he was interrogated before the Sanhedrin, the Jewish Council, condemned to death for blasphemy, and handed over to the Roman governor, Pontius Pilate. Faced with the Sanhedrin's allegation that Jesus claimed to be King of the Jews and was therefore guilty of high treason, Pilate eventually condemned him to be crucified. Jesus was taken out to the place called Golgotha, and crucified. After his death on the cross that Friday, his body was taken down, washed, and laid before nightfall and the beginning of Shabbat in a rock-cut tomb nearby. It was from this tomb, according to the Gospels, that Jesus Christ rose from the dead.

For this original tomb in which Joseph of Arimathea laid Jesus' body on the evening of the day of crucifixion in A.D. 30 or, less likely, 33 we have the direct evidence only of the Gospels. Their accounts are not entirely consistent. Matthew (27:32 to 28:8), Mark (15:20 to 16:8), and Luke (23:26 to 24:10, and 24:22–4) describe the crucifixion and burial in broadly similar terms, but John (19:17 to 20:12) is in some ways more detailed:

(19:17) And he bearing his cross went forth into a place called the place of a skull, which is called in the Hebrew Golgotha, (18) where they crucified him. . . . (19) And Pilate wrote a title and put it on the cross. . . . (20) This title then read many of the Jews, for the place where Jesus was crucified was nigh to the city. . . . (38) And after this Joseph of Arimathea . . . (39) [and] Nicodemus [came] . . . (40) and took the body of Jesus, and wound it in linen clothes with . . . spices, as the manner of Jews is to bury. (41) Now in the place where he was crucified there was a garden; and in the garden a new sepulchre, wherein was never man yet laid. (42) There laid they Jesus therefore because of the Jews' preparation day; for the sepulchre was nigh at hand.

(20:1) The first day of the week cometh Mary Magdalen early . . . unto the sepulchre, and seeth the stone taken away from the sepulchre. . . . (3) Peter . . . went forth . . . and came to the sepulchre. (4) . . . and the other disciple outran Peter and came first to the sepulchre. (5) And he stooping down, and looking in, saw the linen clothes lying; yet went he not in. (6) Then cometh Simon Peter . . . and went into the sepulchre. (10) Then the disciples went away again unto their own home. (11) But Mary stood without at the sepulchre weeping; and as she wept, she stooped down, and looked into the sepulchre, (12) And seeth two angels in white sitting, the one at the head, and the other at the feet, where the body of Jesus had lain. . . .

The essential facts seem to be these. The place of crucifixion, Golgotha, was outside but near to the city in a cultivated area (a "garden") where many could watch and

read the title on Jesus's cross. In that place, near to the place of crucifixion, there was a new tomb, not previously used for burial. The other Gospels add that it was the tomb of a rich member of the council, Joseph of Arimathea, newly cut in the rock and closed by a large stone that could be rolled against, or away from, the door. To look into the tomb, it was necessary to stoop, suggesting a low door. Within, as the other Gospels make clear, there was room for at least five persons, two of whom might be sitting. On the right-hand side, as Mark says, it was possible to sit where the body of Jesus had lain.

A modern Greek wall mosaic behind the Unction Stone at the entrance to the Holy Sepulchre. The mosaic shows the removal of the body of Christ after the crucifixion, the anointment and the preparation of the body, and the burial of Christ in the tomb. Note the skull under the cross.

This kind of tomb is consistent with what we know of contemporary burial practice in the Jerusalem area: a rock-cut tomb, a low entrance closed by a movable stone, and a raised burial shelf within. The problem is that such a tomb is too simple: most tombs of this period had burial shelves on more than one side, long narrow rectangular niches or loculi (*kokhim*) in which a body might be inserted at right angles to the walls of the tomb, and multiple chambers. The absence of such features in the Gospels may be due to the brevity of their accounts: such features were irrelevant, but that does not mean that some of them may not have existed. We cannot be certain, therefore, of the precise type of tomb implied by the Gospel accounts.

If we limit ourselves to what can be derived from the Gospel accounts and to the parallels provided by the contemporary rock-cut tombs of the Jerusalem area, we can reconstruct the probable original form of the rock-cut tomb. The tomb consisted of only two components: an unroofed or partly covered rock-cut forecourt opening by a low entrance into a fully enclosed rock-cut tomb chamber. The entrance to the tomb chamber from the forecourt was closed by a large stone. There is no evidence that this was round: it is more likely to have been roughly dressed and to have been trundled rather than rolled across the entrance. There were probably rock-cut burial shelves on two or three sides of the original burial chamber. The form of the chamber as preserved since 325–326 and still today inside the Edicule, with only a single burial shelf, would be quite exceptional among the one thousand or so rock-cut tombs of the Second Temple period now recorded in the Jerusalem area, among which chambers with two or three shelves predominate. There is no evidence that the burial shelf was set within a niche below the neatly rounded arch of a rock-cut arcosolium. The burial chamber was thus a square or rectangular room with a flat roof, with burial shelves arranged along three sides, and with only a limited space excavated to floor level between the shelves. This deeper area, sometimes called the "standing pit," allowed the burial attendants, bone gatherers, and other visitors to stand upright within the tomb.

Although no part of the rock-cut tomb within the Edicule has been seen since 1809, a series of observations and investigations beneath the Church of the Holy Sepulchre over the past century has revealed something of its original surroundings. The

The traditional tombs of Joseph of Arimathea and Nicodemus located in the Syrian Orthodox chapel at the back of the Rotunda. These tombs, dated to the time of Christ, provide clear evidence that the tomb of Christ was part of a Jewish burial ground in his time.

rocky limestone hillside, which falls steeply from west to east, had been extensively quarried, perhaps for centuries, long before the area was used for burial. Tomb chambers were then cut into the slope of the hill and into the sides of the quarries. Several of these tombs have been recorded, showing that the area was in use as a Jewish cemetery at the time of the death and burial of Jesus. The existence of this cemetery provides a context for his burial and is one of the most remarkable indications of the authenticity of the site.

Golgotha seems to have been an isolated pillar of rock standing out from one of the quarry faces some forty-five meters (148 feet) southeast of the tomb. This closeness is reflected in St. John's Gospel by his statements that the place of crucifixion was near to the sepulchre and was in a garden in the place where he was crucified. As for the word "garden," this means only a cultivated area, such as one finds even today all round Jerusalem in and between the exposures of rock on steep hillsides.

Golgotha and the Tomb in Roman Times
A.D. 30–325

Almost nothing is known of Golgotha or the tomb during the century that elapsed between the crucifixion and the foundation of the Roman colony of Aelia Capitolina on the site of Jerusalem by the Roman emperor Hadrian in 130. In 41–44 Herod Agrippa had extended the city to the northwest bringing the site of Golgotha and the tomb within the walls. This is why the place of crucifixion and the tomb lie today, as they have done ever since, deep inside the city.

The rock-cut tombs on the site of what is now the Church of the Holy Sepulchre must have been emptied and purified by the priests when the city was expanded over them, but we do not know how this expansion affected the Tomb of Christ. The impact on Golgotha and the tomb of the siege and destruction of the city by the Romans under Titus in A.D. 70, and again following their suppression of the Jewish revolt under Bar Kochba in 132–135, is likewise unknown. They may well have been unaffected.

There is one possible reference in the Bible that may reflect the realization that the place of crucifixion now lay within the city. In Revelation 11:8 it is stated that the bodies of the two witnesses "shall lie in the street of the great city which is spiritually called Sodom and Egypt, where [the] Lord was crucified." The "great city" is here the earthly Jerusalem and the phrase takes the tradition of the location of the site inside the city back to the time in the late first century when Revelation was written, and when the site of the crucifixion did indeed already lie within the extended city of 41–44.

The foundation of Colonia Aelia Capitolina by the Roman Emperor Hadrian in 129 or 130, on the ruins of the city destroyed in 70, brought major changes to the area of Golgotha and the tomb. Hadrian's works seem to have begun after the suppression of the Bar Kochba revolt in 135, but our evidence for them relates to the tomb discovered in 325–326, the tomb that lies today beneath the Church of the Holy Sepulchre.

Eusebius, bishop of Caesarea ca. 315–339, the "father of church history," who was a contemporary observer of Hadrian's buildings as they still existed in the 320s, of their removal, and of what was revealed beneath them, is a witness of outstanding importance.

According to his *Life of Constantine*, the whole site had been covered with a great quantity of earth and paved with stone, and on this a temple to Aphrodite (Venus) had been erected over the "sacred cave," i.e. the tomb. Jerome, the translator of the Bible, a monk at Bethlehem from 386 until his death in 420, adds the information that this situation had lasted from the time of Hadrian to the reign of the emperor Constantine, but asserts that it was a statue of Jupiter that had stood over the place of resurrection (again, the tomb) and a statue of Venus on the Rock of the Cross. This confusion may be due to Eusebius who, in his *Life of Constantine*, attributed the temple to Aphrodite in 337–339, more than ten years after its demolition. The coins of Aelia Capitolina — by contrast, strictly contemporary evidence — depict neither Venus nor her temple. They show instead two different temples of Tyche.

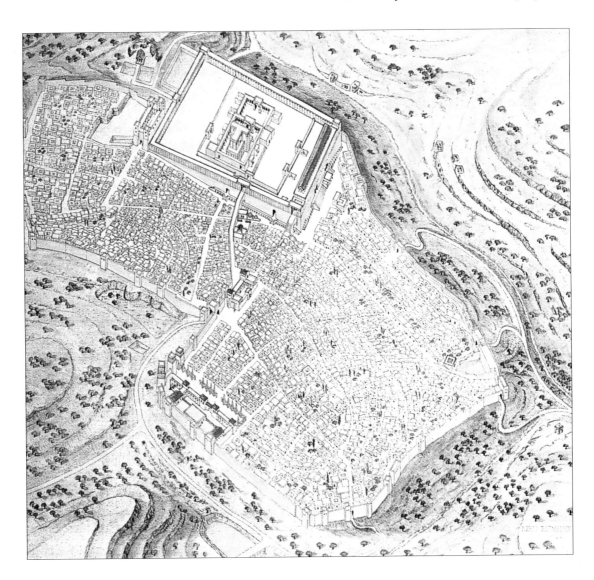

Reconstruction of Jerusalem in the time of Christ, bird's-eye view looking northeast.
At the top of the picture one can see the Temple Mount, enlarged and enriched by King Herod. To the left of the Temple Mount is the Antonia fortress, probably the site of the trial of Jesus. At the bottom left of the picture is the palace and citadel of King Herod. Slightly above it, and outside the walls, is the quarry within which Jesus was crucified.

Eusebius may have chosen to identify one of these with Venus to heighten the supposed defilement of the site. For Jews and Christians, Tyche was a "bearable" pagan deity who even appears on coins of Agrippa II; Aphrodite/Venus was an abomination. The Christian sources go further and accuse Hadrian of a desire to conceal and dishonor the sites of the crucifixion and burial of Jesus, but this seems more likely to reflect fourth-century assumptions about pagan attitudes toward Christianity than second-century reality.

The contribution of archaeological research to the resolution of this problem has been limited. There is evidence for the existence during the Roman era of a large building on the site now occupied by the Church of the Holy Sepulchre, but it is doubtful if it can be precisely dated or more closely identified, except as a monumental public structure. There is certainly not enough archaeological evidence on its own to establish the former existence of a temple on the site of the tomb. One of the most enigmatic finds associated with this period is a polished stone which was discovered at the Chapel of St. Vartan in the crypt of St. Helena. It depicts a crude image of a ship, and a Latin inscription reading "Lord, we have gone."

By putting the accounts of Eusebius and Jerome together with the evidence of the Roman building we can advance a few steps. A consensus is emerging among scholars that Hadrian built the capitol of his new colony, whether deliberately or not, over the site of Golgotha and the tomb. The capitol of a colony, like *the* Capitol in Rome, was the temple of the most important gods of the state, the "Capitoline Triad" of Jupiter, Juno and Minerva. The presence of this temple in Aelia is reflected in the name of the colony, Aelia (from Hadrian's family name) Capitolina, and by its appearance on the coins minted in the city for Hadrian and his successor, Antoninus Pius.

A capitoline temple was always placed on a high point with a view over the city,

reflecting again the location of the Capitol in Rome. The site of Golgotha and the tomb enjoyed such a view over the colony spread out to the east. The remains discovered under the Church of the Holy Sepulchre can be seen in this light as the walls supporting a high podium of the kind which we can infer existed from Eusebius's description of the paving and soil that had to be removed. As for the presence of a statue of Aphrodite/Venus, it was normal for the enclosure of such a capitoline temple to include secondary shrines, so that a statue of a goddess on top of Golgotha, as described by Jerome, is by no means an impossibility, even if it seems more likely (and more appropriately) to have been the goddess Tyche, representing, beside the national cult of Jupiter, the local cult of the good fortune, the "Luck" of Aelia.

In the years between 135 and 325–326 we have two contemporary witnesses to the existence of knowledge of the site of the crucifixion: the sermon *Peri Pascha*, "On Easter," by bishop Melito of Sardis who died toward the end of the second century, and the *Onomastikon* of Eusebius, written probably before the close of the third century.

Peri Pascha, a dramatic work of Greek rhetoric possibly composed between 160 and 170, shows how the Passover narrative of Exodus 12 is to be seen in the light of Christ, the true Passover lamb, the Jewish festival becoming the Christian Easter. In the second half of the sermon, after describing the death of Jesus as the slaughter of the Paschal Lamb, Melito asks, "And where has he been murdered?" and replies, "In the middle of Jerusalem." Melito repeats his charge three times: "you killed your Lord in the middle of Jerusalem," adding "in the middle of the street and in the middle of the city." Melito uses the Greek word *plateia*, meaning a broad street, a word which in the second century was beginning in both Greek and Latin to take on its modern Greek meaning of "square." Melito had apparently learned that the site of the crucifixion was then believed to be in the middle of the city (possibly echoing Revelation 11:8, which also uses the word *plateia*). Melito had gone to the East at some point in his life to investigate the canon of the Old Testament and it was perhaps in the course of this journey that he obtained information about the site of the crucifixion. He must have known that the Gospel of St. John, from which he quotes repeatedly, placed the execution near to (that is, outside) the city (19:20), and that the other Gospels implied this, and that there was therefore a conflict between these accounts and the site he chose to emphasize. His choice heightened the drama of his sermon: we must beware of applying a modern preference for topographical precision.

The Jerusalem ship. A crude image of a ship, and a Latin inscription underneath it reading "Lord, we have gone." The drawing was found on a polished stone in the Chapel of St. Vartan.

*Portrait of Emperor Hadrian
on a bronze coin commemorating
Hadrian's visit to Judea in
130-131. The Israel Museum,
Jerusalem.*

*Roman coin with a symbolic scene
representing the foundation
of Aelia Capitolina by Hadrian,
130-138. The Israel Museum,
Jerusalem.*

What mattered then and now is that in Melito's days the site was apparently identified as lying in the heart of the city, in the middle of a broad paved street or square.

Toward the end of the period between 135 and 325–326 there is a second contemporary witness to the survival of knowledge of the place where Christ was crucified. In his description of the discoveries of 325–326 and of the buildings that Constantine erected, Eusebius failed to mention Golgotha, but in his *Onomastikon*, probably compiled in the 290s, he does have an entry for Golgotha:

> "place of a skull," where the Christ was crucified, which is pointed out in Aelia to the north of Mount Sion.

This location of Golgotha in the Roman colony of Aelia reflects the tradition explicit in Melito that the site of the crucifixion was thought to lie inside the city. This is even more striking because Eusebius used here the Greek word *deiknutai*, "is shown," "is pointed out," with the clear implication that there was something to be seen. The summit of the rock of Golgotha was perhaps visible in the court of the Roman temple erected on the site, perhaps as the base of the cult statue of Venus (or more likely Tyche), but this can be no more than conjecture. What is important is that the place name Golgotha was a landmark to guide the excavations that led to the uncovering of Golgotha and the discovery of the tomb.

Constantine the Great and the Building of the Church
A.D. 325–335

On 28 October 312 Constantine, emperor in the West, defeated his rival Maxentius, emperor in Italy and Africa, at the battle of the Milvian Bridge outside Rome. Following instructions received in a dream the previous night, Constantine fought under the sign of the cross, and attributed his victory to the Christian God. A year later, now senior emperor of the West, Constantine and his colleague Licinius, emperor of the East, agreed on a policy of toleration and freedom of religious worship for all. With the "Peace of the Church," enshrined in the so-called Edict of Milan, persecution of the Christians ceased and the possessions of their churches were restored.

Twelve years later in 324 Constantine defeated his co-emperor Licinius at the battle of Chrysopolis (now Scutari, opposite Istanbul). Sole master of the Roman world, Constantine now increasingly saw himself as entrusted with a divine mission to create a Christian empire. Such an empire demanded a new Christian capital. Barely six weeks after his victory at Chrysopolis, Constantine himself traced out the line of the walls at the consecration of the new city he named after himself, Constantinople.

The following year Constantine summoned a council to settle the Arian Controversy, a dispute about the Person of Christ. It was probably at this council held at Nicea (now Iznik) that the emperor instructed Makarios, bishop of Jerusalem (314–333), to search for the Tomb of Christ buried below the podium of the temple erected by Hadrian in the pagan colony of Aelia Capitolina. Eusebius records in his *Life of Constantine* how the site had been covered to a great depth by a rubble of stones and timbers. When the rubble was removed, "against all expectation the revered and all-hallowed testimony of the Saviour's resurrection was itself revealed," that is, the tomb where the body of Jesus had lain and where he had risen from the dead. The phrase "against all expectation" should probably be taken at face value. The landmark was Golgotha, because it was in some way visible and able to be pointed out. Neither Eusebius in the *Onomastikon* nor Melito in *Peri Pascha* mention the tomb, but the Gospels make it clear that the places of crucifixion and burial were not far apart (see preceding chapter). Nevertheless, the tomb had not been seen for nearly two hundred years and Makarios and Eusebius can have had little reason to suppose that it would have survived and actually be found.

What was found? Eusebius says only that it was a "cave," but Cyril (bishop of Jerusalem, ca. 351–386), who may himself as a boy have seen the cave when first uncovered, provides in his *Catechetical Lectures*, delivered in 348 or 350, a few more details. There was originally a place hollowed out in the rock in front of the entrance to the tomb, but this had been cut away to make room for the imperial adornment. This hollowed-out place would have been an open and unroofed or partly unroofed forecourt or antechamber cut in the rock face, a feature often seen in Jewish tombs of the period in the Jerusalem

Ampullae showing the Edicule below the Rotunda.
The ampullae were probably sold to pilgrims as mementos of their visit to the Holy Land.

Θ ΚΩΝ ϹΤΑΝΤΙΝΟ   ΗΑΓΙΑ ΕΛΕΝΗ

Emperor Constantine and his mother Helena holding the True Cross which by tradition was found by Helena in Jerusalem. Detail of a wall mosaic from the 11th century at Hosious Loukas Monastery, Greece.

area, as Cyril himself points out. When Cyril spoke, the stone that had closed the tomb was still lying before the entrance, and a part of it is preserved today in the altar in the Chapel of the Angel inside the Edicule. Eusebius gives no reasons for his confident identification of the cave thus uncovered as "testimony of the Saviour's resurrection." How was it obvious that this was the tomb of the Gospels? There is no way of knowing. Among a number of tombs uncovered, this one may have appeared to conform to the type of tomb described in the Gospels and, being close to the rock identified as Golgotha, was at once accepted as the authentic tomb. But there could have been more. During the period from the crucifixion down to the moment when it was covered up by Hadrian's building works in 135 the tomb probably remained accessible and — more particularly before 70 — could have been marked, possibly with cut or painted graffiti that were still legible in 325–326 and left no doubt in the minds of those who made the identification. Graffiti are the earliest evidence for the identification of the tomb of Peter in the Vatican cemetery. Graffiti or traces of them may survive on the remains of the tomb in Jerusalem, hidden within the present Edicule.

What was done to the tomb thus discovered? Writing shortly after the discovery, Eusebius recorded in his book *The Theophany* his astonishment that it was then possible to see the rock containing the tomb "standing erect and alone in a level land, and having only

one cavern within it." Cyril added that the antechamber of the tomb had been cut away in the course of the works. From these accounts we can see how the rock had been cut back, leaving only the living rock actually containing the burial chamber to rise as an isolated block from a level surface. Constantine decorated this now free-standing feature "with superb columns and full ornamentation, brightening the solemn cave with all kinds of art-work."

In essence, Constantine built a "little house," known in this and all its subsequent forms as "the Edicule" (from the Latin *aedicula*), to enclose and protect the rock-cut tomb chamber released from the surrounding rock. Constantine's Edicule consisted of two parts. In front was a porch of four columns with a pediment and a gabled roof replacing the rock-cut forecourt. Behind was the tomb-chamber, freed on all sides from the living rock, rounded or polygonal outside, covered with marble, decorated by five columns with semidetached bases and capitals, and surmounted by a conical roof of tapering panels, topped with a cross. These elements were later described by pilgrims and can be seen in various contemporary representations, such as the painted lid of a relic box from the Lateran, or in the pewter flasks from Monza and Bobbio, but they are reflected above all in the great replica carved in Pyrenean marble found at Narbonne in southwest France, and perhaps dating from as early as the fifth century.

The discovery and embellishment of the tomb was only a small part, albeit the most important element, of what Constantine built at the sites of Christ's passion and resurrection. His buildings comprised a five-aisled basilica, a great Rotunda over the Edicule, courts, and porticos. We know, from a letter he wrote to Bishop Makarios (quoted by Eusebius in his *Life of Constantine*), that Constantine had entrusted the building and decoration of the whole complex to Dracillianus, his representative in the East, and to the governor of Palestine. Together these great officials were to provide craftsmen and laborers, and everything else Makarios needed. Columns and marble were to be supplied from all sources by the emperor's direct command, for "it is right that the world's most miraculous place should be worthily embellished." Later sources record that the architect was Zenobius, assisted by the priest Eustathius whose task seems to have been to reach an understanding with the clergy and ascetics of Jerusalem on the liturgical uses for which the building was to be designed. Both were from Constantine's nascent city of Constantinople, and both were perhaps members of the imperial staff bringing that city into being.

Artist's reconstruction of Constantine's church. The huge church, inaugurated in A.D. 335, contained three main sections: a) a basilical church, known as the Marturion (testimony), which was composed of a central nave facing a monumental apse, and two aisles on each side of the nave; b) an inner courtyard, known as Triportico, stretched to the east of the basilica and surrounded by columns from three sides. The rock of the Calvary or Golgotha was preserved near the southeast corner of the courtyard; c) a monumental circular structure, known as the Rotunda or Anastasis (resurrection), built around the Holy Sepulchre.

Artist's reconstruction of Constantine's Edicule which consisted of two parts: in front was a porch of four columns with a pediment and gabled roof. Behind was the tomb-chamber, freed on all sides from the living rock. The tomb-chamber was rounded or polygonal on the outside, and surmounted by a conical roof, topped with a cross. In the interior, covered with marble, were fine columns standing on semidetached bases, and adorned with capitals.

Early in the work, in 327/328, the empress Helena, mother of the emperor Constantine, made an imperial progress to the eastern provinces including Palestine. She would have inspected the works in Jerusalem, and probably provided funds and endowment from the imperial chest, but the initiative for the building of the churches was her son's, not hers. In his *Life of Constantine*, written in 337, Eusebius associates her name with the Church of the Nativity at Bethlehem and the church on the Mount of Olives, but he gives her no role in connection with the works at Golgotha. Fifty years later the pilgrim Egeria was told that Helena had contributed to the magnificence of all Constantine's Holy Land churches. Timbers identified as coming from the True Cross were found in the course of Constantine's works at Golgotha, perhaps at a very early stage when the podium of the pagan temple was being removed and when Eusebius himself records without comment the discovery of timbers. But Bishop Cyril, who has much to say of these relics of the True Cross, nowhere attributes their discovery to Helena. As Hunt, who recently studied the Early Christian pilgrimage to the Holy Land, concludes:

> Helena was carrying into effect the public program of a Christian government, one which took physical shape in the building and adornment of churches. At its heart ... was her sojourn in Jerusalem, and the building works there reflecting the glory of the Christian regime which she shared with her son and grandsons.

Round this very real core of imperial patronage, later centuries were to weave the story of Helena's discovery of the True Cross and of her part in its identification, one of the most widespread and beautiful of all the stories of the medieval church.

We can see Constantine's church buildings vividly displayed on the mosaic map of Jerusalem from Madaba in Jordan. In the bird's-eye view of the map, they form a line of buildings running west from the colonnaded *cardo*, the main street of Roman and Byzantine Jerusalem, and consist of an elaborate entrance, a large building with a gabled roof, the Marturion basilica, and at the west end a large dome rising high above the other structures. Seen in more detail by the visitor entering from the street, there was first a flight of steps and then triple gates leading into a large forecourt or atrium. Most of this area was obliterated by later structures, but fragments of the entrance can still be seen behind

Zelatimo's pastry shop in Khan es-Zeit Street and in the Russian Orthodox Hospice. On the far side of the atrium three more doors opened into the nave and aisles of the five-aisled basilica that would later become known as the Marturion. The basilica was "an extraordinary structure raised to an immense height and very extensive in length and breadth," as Eusebius tells us in the sermon he gave at its dedication in 335. The large building, measuring approximately 40 by 58 meters (131 by 190 feet), was constructed of a nave flanked by two aisles on each side. The aisles were lined with rows of columns and square pillars, with galleries above. A gabled lead roof supported by wooden rafters covered the nave. The ceilings of the nave and aisles were made of gold-plated coffers. Constantine himself suggested that the ceiling should be coffered and decorated with gold and Eusebius described it spreading out "like a vast sea." The altar was at the west end of the basilica, "the chief point of the whole," nearest to Golgotha and the tomb, and was set in a hemisphere (an apse) "ringed with twelve columns to match the number of the Apostles of the Saviour, their tops decorated with great bowls made of silver, which the Emperor himself had presented to his God as a superb offering." The apse was not centered on the tomb itself, but rather on the place where it was later believed the True Cross had been found. The name given to the basilica — the Marturion, "The Testimony" — has led scholars in recent years to believe that the basilica was built in honor of the True Cross, the "token of that holiest Passion," as Constantine himself seems to refer to it in his letter to Bishop Makarios. If this is correct, Constantine's buildings celebrated within one complex the three most holy sites: the place of crucifixion, the place of resurrection, and the place of the finding of the True Cross.

Passing westwards through doors to either side of the apse of the basilica, the pilgrim reached a square courtyard surrounded by porticoes. At its southeast corner the Rock of Golgotha rose on high. Here by the early fifth century there stood under the open sky a large cross adorned with gold and jewels. Across the far side of this "court before the cross," was the entrance to the vast domed Rotunda covering the Edicule erected over the rock-cut tomb. The dome is clearly visible on the Madaba map and although there has been some doubt whether it was actually completed by Constantine, it seems most unlikely that the

The outer wall of the Constantinian Church and the steps leading from the Cardo were exposed in the Russian Hospice.

The earliest known map of Jerusalem was discovered as part of a mosaic pavement showing the sites of the Holy Land in the town of Madaba in Transjordan. The map, dated to the 6th -7th century, shows the city after the construction of the Cardo (the colonnaded main street) laid in the time of Emperor Justinian. The Holy Sepulchre, which dominates the central part of the map, can be seen upside down below the Cardo.

emperor would have failed to complete his work by the construction of the Rotunda and dome over the very structure, the tomb, that Eusebius described as "the head of the whole," "a tomb full of age-long memory, comprising the trophies of the great Saviour's defeat of death, a tomb of divine presence." As completed in 335, two years before the emperor's death, the Marturion basilica had been designed by Constantine to surpass all others, if not in size then in the richness of its marble and decoration. The whole complex of buildings that came later to be called the Church of the Holy Sepulchre would have been in the high style of late Roman architecture, but with the buildings for the most part long vanished there is little on which to base more detailed conclusions. The Edicule above the tomb, to judge by the Narbonne model, seems to have been modelled on a building very similar to the Round Temple at Baalbek in the Bek'aa valley, and it is to this level of imperial competence and elaboration that the whole complex probably conformed.

Constantine's great basilica was probably dedicated on 13 September 335, an event still celebrated each year with an octave of ceremonies which include the feast of the Exaltation of the Cross on 14 September (27 September in the Gregorian calendar). But the 13 September, the Ides of September, "coincides with that of the ancient Roman festival of Jupiter Optimus Maximus, the presiding deity of Hadrian's Aelia Capitolina, now displaced by the revelation of Christ's tomb and the building of the new Jerusalem." As Hunt suggests, this was perhaps intended by Constantine as "a pointed allusion to the expulsion of the pagan gods." It is also a powerful indication that the Roman building demolished and replaced by Constantine's buildings had indeed been the capitoline temple of Roman Aelia.

Of all this great complex only a little survives. The foundations and lower courses of the walls of the original basilica were discovered in several places in and around the church, and a section of the original apse was unearthed in the course of excavations beneath the Katholikon. The enclosing wall of the rotunda, based on bedrock, has been preserved intact in some sections to a height of more than 10 meters (33 feet). The inner face of the wall, covered with marble slabs, is circular, while the outer contour is polygonal. In the wall were three large apses, each illuminated through an arched window.

Pilgrimage and Survival
A.D. 335–1009

For the next two centuries the Church of the Holy Sepulchre stood intact in all its original splendor. This was the period when magnificent churches with superb mosaic floors were being built throughout Palestine, and it is one of these floors at Madaba (now in Jordan) that gives us the most vivid impression of what the Church of the Holy Sepulchre looked like when visited by the earliest pilgrims. Some of these were great ladies, such as the empress Helena herself, who had come at the very beginning of the work, and the empress Eudocia, wife of Theodosius II (402–450), who at the wish of her husband embarked on pilgrimage to Palestine a century later in the spring of 438. A learned and cultured Byzantine lady, she made lavish imperial donations to the churches on her route, and in Jerusalem she was present at the dedication of a new shrine to house the relics of St. Stephen outside the city's northern gate. She must have visited the Church of the Holy Sepulchre in great state and made ample gifts, but sadly we know nothing of this. Two decades earlier her husband Theodosius had erected on Mount Calvary a great, richly jeweled golden cross. This appears on his gold coins supported by a figure of Victory; on the coinage of Tiberius II (578–582) and his successors it stands on a series of steps, representing the hill of Golgotha.

It is pilgrims of lesser rank who have left us some account of what they saw. The earliest of those we know came from Bordeaux in 333, while the Church of the Holy Sepulchre was still being built. He mentions the little hill of Golgotha,

> where the Lord was crucified, and about a stone's throw from it the vault where they laid his body, and he rose again on the third day. By the order of the Emperor Constantine there has now been built there a basilica, the house of the Lord, and beside it cisterns of wonderful beauty, and to the rear a bath where children are baptized.

This is a frustratingly short description, omitting much, but also including two elements — the cisterns and baptistery — of which nothing else is known.

Far more informative was another pilgrim from the furthest west, Egeria, a pious lady from Galicia in northwest Spain who spent the years 381–384 in the Holy Land. By her time, the great feast commemorating the dedication of Constantine's basilica in September 335 had settled into the regular pattern of the church's year in Jerusalem. Egeria provides a partial account of this feast that breaks off after describing the first two of the eight days of special liturgy. Before this, however, Egeria gives us a unique picture of the daily services in the Church of the Holy Sepulchre just half a century after its construction. She describes how the doors of the Anastasis, the circular church around the

A detail of the Madaba Map showing the church of the Holy Sepulchre. The map clearly shows a series of steps rising up to the facade of the basilica. The dome of the Rotunda can be seen towering above the roof of the basilica.

tomb, were opened before cockcrow each day, and how the people entered to sing and pray until the bishop came at dawn with his clergy. The bishop entered the tomb and standing inside "the screen," in the portico of the Edicule, said the first prayers and blessed the faithful.

Egeria was fascinated by the building and its decoration:

> The decorations really are too marvellous for words. All you can see is gold and jewels and silk; the hangings are entirely silk with gold stripes, the curtains the same, and everything they use for services at the festival is made of gold and jewels. You simply cannot imagine the number, and the sheer weight of the candles and the tapers and lamps and everything else they use for the services.

Egeria goes on to describe the rest of the services held each weekday at the Anastasis and at the cross on the hill of Golgotha. On Sundays the services again began before dawn at the Anastasis and continued at the cross. At daybreak the people assembled in the Great Church, the Marturion basilica, for the principal liturgy of the week, during which a priest or priests might preach and the bishop delivered a sermon. The service lasted until midmorning, and was followed by a return to the Anastasis for thanksgiving and prayers, where the bishop concluded the proceedings by blessing the people. As he left, everyone came to kiss his hand. Egeria then proceeds through the liturgical year, beginning on 6 January at Epiphany, the feast celebrating the baptism of Jesus, continuing through the Great Week of Easter (and the preparation of those who were about to be baptised), and finishing with the rest of the Christian year. She then begins to describe the days of the feast of Encaenia, celebrating the dedication of the church some fifty years before, but it is here that the surviving text of her incomparable account comes to an end.

One of Egeria's most moving accounts relates to Easter Friday:

> It is impressive to see the way all the people are moved by these readings, and how they mourn. You could hardly believe how every single one of them weeps during the three hours, old and young alike, because of the manner in which the Lord suffered for us.

Few other pilgrims wrote accounts of what they saw and did, and even fewer of their accounts have survived. But the pilgrims must have come in their thousands. A local industry grew up to provide them with mementos of the holy places: pewter medallions; pewter flasks to contain holy oil from the tomb, like those now surviving in the treasuries of Monza and Bobbio; wooden boxes closed by a painted wooden lid and containing pieces of rock and soil from the tomb, from Golgotha, and from many other sacred places. One example of such a box survives, found in the treasure of the Lateran in Rome and now preserved in the Museo Sacro of the Biblioteca Apostolica in the Vatican. There may also have been models of the church, or at least of its individual parts, for pilgrims to buy and take home. None of these is known to survive, but something like this must lie behind the copy of the Edicule, over 1.24 meters (4 feet) high, carved in Pyrenean marble, now preserved in the Musée d'Art et d'Histoire at Narbonne in southwestern France. Being made of local marble, it can only have been based on drawings or more likely on a model brought back from Palestine. Most of our surviving evidence of what the church looked like relates to the Edicule, some to Golgotha and its cross, as seen on coins and pottery flasks. For the church as a whole, the Rotunda of the Anastasis and the Marturion, we have only the great image on the Madaba mosaic and some archaeological evidence of foundations and walls which allow us to reconstruct in some detail the plan and even the appearance of the whole complex.

Almost two centuries of uninterrupted prayer and worship were brought savagely to an end in A.D. 614. The Persians had invaded the Byzantine empire two years before, had taken Antioch and Damascus, and in 614 attacked Palestine and captured Jerusalem. For three days the Persian commander sacked the city:

> ... who can depict what took place within Jerusalem and in her streets? ... the people in crowds fled into churches and altars; and there [the Persians] destroyed them.... Any that were caught armed, were massacred with their own weapons.... Holy churches were burned with fire, others were demolished, majestic altars fell prone, sacred crosses were trampled underfoot, life-giving icons were spat upon by the unclean. Their wrath fell upon priests and deacons: they slew them in their churches like dumb animals.... How many fled into the Church of the Anastasis, into that of Sion and other churches, and were therein massacred and consumed with fire! Who can count the multitude of the corpses of those who were massacred in Jerusalem!

Despite the hyperbole of Antiochus Strategos's account of the sack of Jerusalem, the evidence is that many thousands were massacred and many thousands taken captive, including Zacharias, the patriarch of Jerusalem, and the Staurophylax, the official who had charge of the relic of the True Cross. The True Cross itself, kept since the time of Constantine in a silver casket said to have been provided by the empress Helena, was taken into captivity beyond the Euphrates. King Chosroes of Persia when he heard what had happened gave order to pardon the captives and rebuild the city. The damage had been done, but it is very difficult to know what it amounted to. Some churches were burnt and never restored, all were probably looted and desecrated, but Modestus, the abbot of St. Theodosius outside Jerusalem, who was left in charge of the city by the Persians, secured financial help from the patriarch of Alexandria and by 625 was able to write that all the Jerusalem churches had been restored. Even if this is an exaggeration, it certainly suggests that the damage was not too serious to be put right. Both the surviving structure of Constantine's Anastasis Rotunda, and the description given by the pilgrim Arculf of the Church of the Holy Sepulchre as it was later in the century (see below) suggest that the basic structure remained standing, even if stripped of valuables and in need of reroofing.

The Byzantine emperor Heraclius struck back in 622. Attacking the Persian empire in what has been called the Last Great War of Antiquity, he recovered the lost provinces, invaded Persia, and recovered the relic of the True Cross. On 21 March 630, Heraclius himself, walking barefoot and in mean attire, carried the relic of the True Cross in solemn procession back into Jerusalem. Still today, every year in Jerusalem, the return of the True Cross is celebrated by the Orthodox in the feast of the Veneration of the Cross held on the third Sunday before Easter.

Four years later, the Muslim armies from Arabia overran Palestine and in 636 Heraclius was defeated at the Battle of Yarmuk. In 638 Sophronios, patriarch of Jerusalem, surrendered the city to Caliph 'Umar. The caliph granted security of person and property to the Christians, and guaranteed the safety of their churches and monasteries, but all who stayed were to pay the poll tax. When the terms of peace had been agreed, 'Umar entered the city. The Commander of the Faithful was dressed as an ordinary bedouin, riding on a camel. He refused to pray either in the Anastasis or the Great Church, the Marturion, but spread his prayer mat in the portico at the east end of the atrium, nearest the cardo. After he had prayed, the caliph is said to have told the patriarch that had he prayed in the Anastasis or the Marturion, his followers would have seized those buildings. Long afterwards, a record of the caliph's supposed action in securing the Anastasis and

The Holy City of Jerusalem.
Detail of a mosaic in the church
of St. Stephen at Kastrom Mefaa
(Um el-Rassas), Jordan.

Marturion against intrusion by Muslims, by prohibiting them from performing their devotions except in the atrium of the Marturion and then one at a time, was inscribed high on the wall at the east end of the atrium of Constantine's church. In Arabic Kufic lettering dating from the tenth century A.D., this inscription is preserved on a ruined fragment of wall visible today in the Russian Orthodox Hospice:

> In the Name of God, the merciful and compassionate. From the Exalted Majesty. It is commanded that this masjid be guarded and that none of those under our protection be allowed to enter it, either for payment or for any other consideration ....

The portico alone was thus secured for individual and solitary, but not congregational Muslim worship. It is perhaps thus from 'Umar's time that the main entrance to the Church of the Holy Sepulchre was moved to the south, to roughly where it is today, the eastern portico being from now on forbidden to the Christians.

For the next four centuries, the Church of the Holy Sepulchre was in continuous and essentially uninterrupted use. Pilgrims visited it in substantial, if reduced numbers, and as

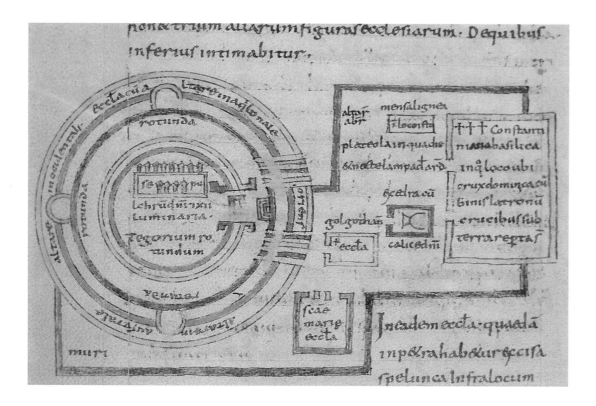

before some wrote accounts of what they saw. The most informative of these accounts were again composed by those from the furthest west. Arculf, a bishop from Gaul, was in Jerusalem sometime between 679 and 682. On his return to his native land he was carried by a storm to the shores of Britain, and reached the island of Iona off the coast of Scotland. There he dictated to Adomnan, abbot of the monastery of Iona, an account of the holy places and drew for him, on little tablets of wax, a remarkable series of plans of the holy buildings, including the Church of the Holy Sepulchre. Adomnan later published Arculf's account in a book titled *On the Holy Places*, in which he included copies of the church plans that Arculf had drawn for him. Arculf describes a round church, the Anastasis, built over and around the tomb of Jesus. The church had twelve columns of great size, three concentric walls, and three altars in recesses in the middle wall. Two other altars, one in front of the tomb door and the other to the east, were originally parts of the stone that had been rolled against the entrance of the Tomb of Christ after his burial (Matthew 27:60; Mark 15:46). In the center of the round church was the sepulchre itself — a small circular building hewn from the rock, its entrance facing east. The exterior was covered with marble, and the roof, decorated with gold, supported a large gold cross. Inside the sepulchre, to the north and carved out of the same rock, was a single shelf where the body of Jesus had been placed. Twelve oil lamps, for the number of the disciples, burned day and night above the shelf.

The rectangular Church of Saint Mary, Mother of Jesus, was recorded by Arculf to the southeast of the round Church of the Anastasis. Another church, which Arculf described as "very large," stood on the site of Golgotha. A great silver cross marked the place where once had stood the wooden cross on which Jesus had been crucified. Below was a cave hewn in the rock, with an altar on which masses were offered for the souls of certain privileged persons. East of the Church of Golgotha was a chapel that contained the cup from which the disciples had drunk at the Last Supper (Matthew 26:27–29; Mark 14:23–25). In the cup was the sponge, which had been dipped in vinegar, put on hyssop, and brought to Jesus's mouth while on the cross, before "he bowed his head and gave up his spirit" (John 19:29–30). Farther east was the Marturion basilica on the site where Jesus's cross had been discovered, together with the crosses of the two thieves. In the portico of the basilica was kept the

A schematic plan of the Holy Sepulchre from a 9th-century manuscript based on Arculf's account of his visit to the Holy Places in the 7th century. On the left is the Edicule surrounded by the Rotunda with its three apses.

lance with which the soldier pierced Jesus's side as he was hanging from the cross (John 19:34). Between the Marturion basilica and the Church of the Anastasis was an open courtyard with lamps burning day and night. A large wooden table stood in the northeast corner of the courtyard, on the site where, according to Arculf, the patriarch Abraham had set up an altar for the sacrifice of his son Isaac (Genesis 22:1–19).

The Englishman Willibald (700–86), later bishop of Eichstätt in Bavaria, visited the Holy Land between 724 and 730, and later dictated a description of the place of the cross and particularly of the rock-cut tomb and Edicule:

And inside there is a shelf on which the Lord's body lay. Fifteen golden bowls stand on the shelf. They are filled with oil and burn day and night. The shelf on which the Lord's body lay is inside the rock of the tomb on the north side, that is, on the right side as one enters the tomb to pray. And there also, in front of the tomb door, lies a large square stone, like the original stone which the angel rolled away from the tomb door.

There are few pilgrim mementoes from these centuries after the Persian attack and the Arab conquest, perhaps because the Christian community in Jerusalem was much reduced and nothing like the pilgrim industry of earlier centuries had survived. There are also fewer pilgrim accounts, especially from the ninth and tenth centuries, but about 870 Bernard the Monk wrote the earliest description we have of the ceremony of the Holy Fire in the Church of the Holy Sepulchre:

It is worth saying what happens on Holy Saturday, the Vigil of Easter. In the morning the office begins in this church. Then, when it is over they go on singing Kyrie alison until an angel comes and kindles light in the lamps which hang above the sepulchre. The patriarch passes some of the light to the bishops and the rest of the people, and thus each one has light where he is standing.

Bernard's words describe the ceremony of the Holy Fire as conducted today, eleven centuries later, as if it were his own. How much earlier the ceremony had begun, we do not know.

Somewhat earlier, in the time of Thomas, patriarch of Jerusalem (809–29), the dome of Constantine's Rotunda of the Anastasis had been reconstructed. It may have retained the dome shown on the Madaba map until this time, but it was Thomas who rebuilt the roof as an open cone, the form it was to preserve through several reconstructions down to 1808. To do this Thomas imported forty large trunks of cedar from Cyprus to make a double cupola, with an inner and outer structure between which there was space for a man to walk upright on top of the wall of the Rotunda.

The Church of the Holy Sepulchre was damaged by riots in 937 and again in 966, but at the end of the first millennium it was still essentially intact as Constantine had built it seven hundred years before.

Destruction and Rebuilding
A.D.1009–1041 and After

Suddenly in 1009, apparently without warning, the Fatimid ruler of Egypt and Palestine, the caliph al-Hakim bi-Amr Allah (996–1021), ordered the governor of Ramla "to demolish the church of the Resurrection and to remove its [Christian] symbols, and to get rid of all traces and remembrance of it." The governor's agents seized the furnishings, and knocked the church down to its foundations, "except for what was impossible to destroy and difficult to grub up to take away." They "worked hard to destroy the tomb and to remove every trace of it, and did in actual fact hew and root up the greater part of it." The caliph's action seems the more irrational because his mother and sister were Christians and his uncle Orestes had been patriarch of Jerusalem (984–1005). The caliph was soon to repent, but the damage had already been done.

News of what had happened soon reached the West. Raoul de Couhé, bishop of Périgueux, reported on his return from Jerusalem in 1010 "the abominable things he had seen," and how the destroyers,

> when they were unable by any means to reduce the tomb to rubble, also tried a great fire, but it remained like adamant, immovable and intact.
>
> Al-Hakim's agents had also used iron hammers to break up the hollow structure of the tomb but had failed to do so. The accounts by Muslim officials, Christian Arab writers, and western clerics all show that the rock-cut tomb at least was not completely demolished.

The destruction of the church as a whole could hardly have been more thorough. Constantine's Great Church of the Marturion was gone, never to be rebuilt. Yet even parts of this church, sections of the entrance, still stand to a height of 5 meters (16 feet) or more inside the Russian Orthodox Hospice, preserving the tenth-century Arabic Kufic inscription protecting the *masjid* where 'Umar had prayed. As for the Rotunda of the Anastasis, much of the outer wall also survived, Constantine's work still standing today to a height of 11 meters (36 feet) or more. But the interior of the Rotunda with its roof, columns, and piers had been brought down, and it was probably the rubble from these which encumbered and hid the lower parts of the outer walls, and protected the lower parts of the Edicule and the rock-cut tomb from al-Hakim's men. The rock-cut roof of the tomb and most of its end walls were broken down, but its south and north walls and above all the burial couch survived.

The caliph was soon persuaded to relent. As early as 1012, only three years after its destruction, the Christians of Jerusalem were able to begin repairing and rebuilding the Rotunda, the Church of the Anastasis, the Resurrection. In 1014, al-Hakim's mother Maria, began "to rebuild with well-dressed squared stones the Temple of Christ destroyed by her son's order." The Rotunda now became the main part of the church, changing for all time the character of the great complex erected by Constantine, and

An arched doorway from the Crusader period that led from the Chapel of the Apparition inside the Holy Sepulchre to the Christian Quarter Street. The arch, commonly known as Mary's Portal, was probably blocked following the conquest of Jerusalem by Saladin in 1187.

setting the future of the building down to our own times.

The Christians were still harassed, however, and in 1020 al-Hakim ordered that their liturgies should be allowed to be celebrated without hindrance "in the enclosure of the church known as the Quyâmah [the Resurrection] and on its ruins." In 1023, two years after al-Hakim's death, the patriarch of Jerusalem went to Constantinople on the instruction of the late caliph's sister, Sitt al-Mulk, to report to the emperor Basil II (976–1025) on the restoration and rebuilding of the Church of the Holy Sepulchre and the other churches that had been destroyed in Palestine, Egypt, and Syria. His embassy seems to mark the completion of the first stage in the rebuilding of the Holy Sepulchre, which lasted some ten years, from 1012 to 1023.

This rebuilding must have been known in the West at the latest by the autumn of 1026 when a great pilgrimage left for Jerusalem and was present at the ceremony of the Holy Fire at Easter 1027. Pilgrimage to the Holy Sepulchre had indeed begun again after only a very short break following the destruction of 1009. The Irish St. Coloman died en route in 1012; Adalgerius, a future abbot of Conques, made the journey before 1019; and Giraud, abbot of Saumur, was beheaded on his way to the Holy Sepulchre in 1022. A Greek monk of Sinai, Symeon, served for seven years as a guide for pilgrims in Jerusalem ca.1012–18 and it seems to have been he who told the pilgrims of 1026–7 that the rebuilt church was not comparable to its predecessor in either beauty or size. Yet the liturgies of Holy Week 1027 were remarkable for their normality: the pilgrims' account of the Holy Fire, might have been written of any Holy Week down to modern times.

The pilgrimage of 1026–7 was only one of the pilgrimages that in the course of the next few years were to mark the millennium of Christ's crucifixion and resurrection, bringing thousands of pilgrims to Jerusalem. Pilgrimage to Jerusalem at that time was sometimes conceived as the crowning achievement of a Christian's earthly life; as described by Rudolf Glaber, a monk of Cluny:

> At the same time from all over the world an innumerable crowd began to flock to the Sepulchre of the Saviour in Jerusalem — in greater numbers than any one had before thought possible. Not only were there some of the common people and of the middle class, but there were also several very great kings, counts, and noblemen. Finally — and this has never happened before — many noble ladies set out with the poor people. Many desired that they might die rather than return home.

The numbers and rank of those involved in the pilgrimages of the 1020s and 1030s, and the many donations they made "for restoring the House of God," suggest that the reconstruction of the Holy Sepulchre from 1012 onwards cannot have been negligible. Among these donations were the pound of gold paid in 1027 for the cup in which the Holy Fire had appeared, and the hundred pounds of gold said to have been sent by Duke Richard II of Normandy "to the tomb of the Saviour at Jerusalem." The ritual of the Holy Fire and the hanging of lamps over the tomb mean that the Edicule must have been rebuilt over whatever remained of the rock-cut tomb. Temporary roofs could have been erected around the inside of the Rotunda, supported by the surviving or re-erected columns and piers of the ambulatory. This, with the rebuilt Edicule, would have been sufficient for both the daily and the special liturgies, but there is no reason why the Rotunda and its roof may not have been fully restored, together with some of the other buildings.

More or less normal relations between Byzantium and the Fatimid caliphs of Cairo were apparently reestablished in 1027, but it was not until 1037/8 that there was a formal agreement between the emperor Michael IV, the Paphlagonian (1034–41), and the caliph al-Mustansir (1036–94). One of the conditions was that the Church of the Resurrection should be rebuilt at the emperor's expense, implying that there was clearly much still to be done. Workmen and "a vast quantity of silver and gold" were sent, but it is usually said that most of the assistance came in the time of the emperor Constantine IX Monomachos (1042–55), and that the work was completed in 1048. This is the view reported by the great Crusader historian, William of Tyre, writing from ca.1165 onwards, more than a century after the event, but Byzantine historians more nearly contemporary with the events all show that this second phase of the eleventh-century rebuilding began ca.1037/8 in the reign of Michael IV and was finished before his death in 1041. None attribute the rebuilding to Constantine IX.

If the reconstruction was complete before the death of Michael IV in 1041, it explains how it was that the Persian traveler Nasir-i-Khusrau, a strictly contemporary witness, saw the church in the spring of 1047 in what sounds like its fully restored state:

> a most spacious building . . . capable of containing eight thousand persons . . . built, with the utmost skill, of coloured marbles, with ornamentation and sculptures, inside . . . everywhere adorned with Byzantine brocade, worked in gold with pictures. . . . There are also pictures [i.e., mosaics] of the Prophets.

Constantine's great basilica, the Marturion, was gone forever, but the places which have always been the goal of pilgrims, Golgotha and the Life-Giving Tomb, were now again readily accessible. The Rotunda had been completely rebuilt, richly decorated but otherwise very much as we see it today, with a circle of columns and piers at ground level, and a great encircling gallery above. The gallery level was connected directly to the Christian Quarter Street through a newly constructed opening. The Rotunda and the galleries were paved by

Details of pavements found in the ambulatory of the Rotunda and dated to the 11th century. Additional pavements of this kind were uncovered in the gallery.

The windows of the reconstructed north transept wall display typical building techniques, brought by the architects from Byzantium in the 11th century.

mosaic and marble floors. Some of the floors were composed of small marble slabs arranged in geometric designs. Other fragments of mosaic floors, discovered in the course of renovations at the Rotunda, contained depictions of birds and fish.

On the east side of the Rotunda, opening eastwards from the huge arch which still stands, the Byzantine rebuilders constructed an apse as the setting for the principal altar of their new church. East of the apse there was an open courtyard surrounded by colonnades, part of which still survives in the so-called Arches of the Virgin in the north aisle of the Crusader church. Three lesser chapels opened eastwards from the east colonnade, and at the southeast corner of the courtyard another chapel rose over the Rock of Golgotha.

The Edicule had also been rebuilt. Like its Constantinian predecessor, the eleventh-century Edicule comprised two principal elements: a rounded western structure enclosing what remained of the tomb chamber and a narrower rectangular eastern compartment providing the entry to the tomb. To these were now added a cupola carried on pillars and set on top of the burial chamber, and a chapel attached to the west end of the Edicule, on the site of the Coptic Chapel of today. At this time too, benches were added flanking the entry in front of the door of the Edicule. The form of this eleventh-century Edicule is very much what we see today, surviving to a remarkable degree through the reconstructions of 1555 and 1809–10.

The reconstructed porch of the tomb, today the Chapel of the Angel, had gates to the north, south, and east. Pilgrims came in through the north gate, entered the tomb, and left through the south gate, the east gate being reserved for the guardians. Inside, the porch was decorated with mosaic, its west wall apsidal and covered by a conch, just as in the Constantinian Edicule and in the Narbonne model of seven centuries before. Over the low entrance to the tomb chamber there was a mosaic showing the entombment and the angel with the three Marys at the empty tomb. Inside the tomb chamber, whatever remained of the rock-cut bench on which the body of Christ had lain was now covered, protected, and hidden from view (as it has been ever since) by marble slabs.

The Crusaders Modify the Church of the Holy Sepulchre A.D. 1099–1187

In 1071 the Byzantine emperor was disastrously defeated by the Seljuk Turks at the Battle of Manzikert in east Turkey. Two years later, pushing down the east coast of the Mediterranean, the Seljuks under the Turkoman warlord Atsiz captured Jerusalem from the Fatimid Arabs. Access to the holy places of Christendom was now severely restricted, and the Byzantine emperors appealed to the West for help. On 27 November 1095 at the Council of Clermont, Pope Urban II called for a crusade:

> The Turks, a Persian race, have overrun the eastern Christians right up to the Mediterranean Sea . . . capturing and slaughtering many, destroying churches and laying waste the kingdom of God. So, if you leave them alone much longer they will further grind under their heels the faithful of God.

Over the next few years several armies left Europe for the East and on 7 June 1099 arrived and encamped outside the walls of Jerusalem. After a siege of five weeks, the Crusaders broke in over the north wall on 15 July and fought their way through the narrow streets:

> It was necessary to pick one's way over the bodies of men and horses . . . in the Temple and porch of Solomon men rode in blood up to their knees and bridle reins. Indeed, it was a just and splendid judgment of God that this place should be filled with the blood of unbelievers, since it had suffered so long from their blasphemies. The city was filled with corpses and blood. . . . Then the clergy and the laity, going to the Lord's Sepulchre and his most glorious Temple, singing a new canticle to the Lord in a resounding voice of exaltation, and making offerings and most humble supplications, joyously visited the holy places as they had long desired to do.

By their own admission the crusaders massacred hundreds, perhaps thousands of the inhabitants, Muslim and Jewish alike, and late in the day went in solemn state through the deserted Christian quarter to give thanks to God in the Church of the Holy Sepulchre. Two days later Godfrey of Bouillon, duke of Lower Lorraine, was elected *Advocatus Sancti Sepulchri*, Defender of the Holy Sepulchre. The Crusaders' capture of the Holy City was a feat of organization and arms that, according to the historian Riley-Smith, "astonished them as much as it did their contemporaries."

The Crusaders now set about the creation of a feudal society on Western lines, complete with an ecclesiastical hierarchy under a Latin patriarch. The Greek Orthodox patriarch, Simeon, and all the upper hierarchy were excluded and the property of the Greek church was taken over by the Crusader church. Only at the lowest level were the Arabic-speaking local clergy allowed to remain in post. The Crusaders took over the offices and property of the Greek Orthodox

The conquest of Jerusalem by the Crusaders in 1099, as described in an illustrated manuscript from the 13th century (William of Tyre, Chronicon). *In the foreground, knights breach the wall of Jerusalem using a siege tower, while in the background are scenes representing some of the Stations of the Cross, including the crucifixion.*

church precisely because they did not regard it as heretical. They simply subsumed it under higher Latin control, allowing a number of monasteries in the neighborhood of Jerusalem to survive and a Greek community under its own head to remain in the Church of the Holy Sepulchre. Crusader policy towards the Oriental churches, notably the Armenians and Jacobites, was perhaps less severe. Services in the Church of the Holy Sepulchre, and even some of its chapels and altars, were reserved for the non-Latin local clergy, but considering that the Crusaders had come to free the Holy Places from Muslim control, their policy towards these eastern churches has to be regarded as a total failure.

Within the year Godfrey had died and had been buried in the Church of the Holy Sepulchre, at the foot of the Rock of Calvary. On Christmas Day 1100 Baldwin of Boulogne, count of Edessa, was crowned king of Jerusalem by the patriarch Daimbert in the Church of the Nativity in Bethlehem. Later practice would be different: all Baldwin's successors were to be crowned and buried in the Church of the Holy Sepulchre, henceforth the principal church of the Kingdom of Jerusalem, the setting of its greatest ceremonials, and its finest architectural achievement.

The Byzantine rebuilding of the church which the Crusaders had thus acquired by conquest had been completed less than sixty years before. It was covered with mosaics, the holy prophets around the high walls of the Rotunda of the Anastasis, Christ Pantocrator in the apse above the great altar. The lower parts of the walls were clad with marble slabs, the floor laid with geometric patterns in black and white marble. There was little that needed doing immediately and little seems to have been done. When the first Russian pilgrim of whom we know, Daniel the Abbot, reached Jerusalem about 1106-1108, he noted in a long description of the church that "the Franks" had placed a larger-than-life-size silver figure of Christ on the cupola of the Edicule. He attributes nothing else to the Crusaders. They seem in fact to have approached the reconstruction of the Church of the Holy Sepulchre with a circumspection amounting almost to timidity, perhaps because they had found a newly built church in good condition, of considerable size, and decorated throughout with the finest mosaics and painting.

There was one exception. In 1105, King Baldwin ordered an inscription in golden letters to be placed in the then still existing Byzantine apse of the Church of the Holy Sepulchre acknowledging the aid that the Italian city of Genoa had given in the conquest of the Holy Land and listing the grants made to her in gratitude. This "Golden Inscription" was destroyed in the time of King Amalric (1163–74), perhaps, as we shall see, because the Byzantine apse was then destroyed to make way for the completion of the Crusader church.

In the early years of the twelfth century, the Crusaders first priority was to erect to the east of the church, on the site of Constantine's Marturion basilica and its atrium, the entire complex of buildings necessary to house the prior and canons of the newly founded Augustinian Priory of the Holy Sepulchre — cloister, chapter house, refectory, kitchen, and dormitory. Deep below the cloister, the Crusaders rebuilt or restored the Chapel of St. Helena and the adjacent and yet lower Chapel of the Finding of the Cross. Both chapels survive, the cupola of the Chapel of St. Helena still rising through the center of the cloister above. But the priory buildings, the cloister, refectory, chapter house, and dormitory are now ruined shells occupied today by the small cells of the Ethiopian monastery. Although said to live on the roof of the church, the Ethiopians live only where the canons themselves lived some eight centuries before. Deep below the ruined buildings to the north of the priory cloister, recent research has discovered still intact vast vaulted substructures belonging to the canons, probably providing storage and perhaps accommodation for pilgrims.

In 1149 the Crusaders completed the first part of their reconstruction of the church itself, the complete rebuilding of the complex of chapels surrounding and enclosing the Rock of Calvary. These comprised, as they do today, two chapels at ground level and two above, level with the top of the rock. The date of 1149 derives from a Latin inscription which could once be read in golden letters on the wall above or around the arch that led to the Chapel of Golgotha (now the Chapel of Adam) below the Chapel of the Exaltation (or Raising) of the Cross, the northern of the two chapels on Calvary. The inscription can be reconstructed and translated to read:

> This place is holy, sanctified by the blood of Christ,
> By our consecration we add nothing to its holiness.
> But the house built around and above this sacred place
> Was consecrated on the fifteenth day of July,
> With other fathers present, by Fulcher the patriarch,
> Who was then in the fourth year of his patriarchate,
> The fiftieth year since the capture of the City,
> Which then shone like pure gold.
> From the birth of the Lord there were numbered
> Eleven hundred and forty and nine years.

After rebuilding the chapels around Calvary, the Crusaders turned to their last and greatest task in the Church of the Holy Sepulchre. Into the open court to the east of the Anastasis — the "court before the cross" of Constantine's original buildings and of their Byzantine successor — they inserted a great presbytery — now the Katholikon — with a two-storied

*To the East of the Katholikon,
down a steep staircase, lies the
Armenian Chapel of St. Helena.
The exterior walls of the chapel
date to the original Constantinian
construction of the church, though
the rest of the edifice should be
dated to the Crusader restoration.*

choir and an eastern apse, behind which is an ambulatory and three radiating chapels. A high
dome on pendentives was built over the crossing, creating — together with the existing
Rotunda dome — a unique two-domed structure. It was a work of virtuoso architectural skill,
in the finest late Romanesque style of central France. This Crusader building settled for all
time the final form of the Church of the Holy Sepulchre, and it survives today very much as it
was built eight centuries ago.

The grand facade of the south transept incorporated the double portal that formed the
principal entrance to the new church, the lintels adorned with some of the greatest of all
Crusader sculptures. Immediately inside, as still today, were the chapels of Calvary, before which
lay the tombs of the kings of Jerusalem, now long since vanished. Immediately outside, and
marking the location of the entrance from afar, rose a five-story campanile, reduced in 1719 to its
present height of three stories, but still competing as it has done for centuries with the minarets
of the Mosque of 'Umar and of the el-Khankah, immediately to south and north.

Scholars have usually dated the completion and consecration of these works to 15 July
1149, the fiftieth anniversary of the capture of the city by the Crusaders, when the Calvary
chapels were indeed dedicated, as we have just seen. But the contemporary Crusader historian
William, archbishop of Tyre, makes no mention of such a dedication. And it has become
increasingly obvious that parts of the church and some of its sculpture belong not to the 1130s
and 1140s but to the 1150s and later. If we look closely at the documents in the archives of the
Crusader Priory of the Holy Sepulchre, we can see that this is what they too suggest. From 1102
up to 1167 the altars and sanctuaries mentioned were always the same from one document to

another: the Holy Sepulchre (i.e., the tomb), the Cross (i.e., Calvary), and two other altars. But in a document of 1169 and from then onwards there were added: the high altar in the choir, the prison and its altar, the Invention (i.e., the chapel of the Finding of the Cross) and its altars, the parochial altar behind the tomb, the patriarchal throne behind the high altar, and the Compas in the middle of the choir. This charter of 1169 reflects the church as we know it today, for the Compas, the Middle of the World, is now inside the church, in the Greek Katholikon, whereas previously it had been outside in the open court to the east of the Rotunda and its Byzantine apse, while the prison and the Invention of the Cross now communicate directly with the interior of the building. So between 1167 and 1169, the documents begin to reflect a profound rearrangement of the church.

Already 140 years ago a French scholar, Melchior de Vogüé, had noted other evidence to the same effect. The first four kings of Jerusalem, up to Fulk of Anjou, who died in 1143, were buried next to Godfrey of Bouillon at the foot of the Calvary chapels. When Baldwin III died in 1163 he was buried instead between the piers on the south side of the crossing of the Crusader church. Another pointer is provided by the destruction in the time of King Amalric (1163–74) of the "Genoese Golden Inscription" in the apse of the Byzantine church, something which can only have taken place when the Byzantine apse was demolished to open up the Rotunda to the presbytery and east end of the new Crusader church. For John of Würzburg, who visited Jerusalem about 1170, the choir was then, "the addition of a new church." He continues with repeated emphasis, "a new structure and recently added . . . in which the high altar is consecrated in honour of the Anastasis, the Holy Resurrection." It looks therefore as if, as in countless churches of the West, the old work had been allowed to stand and worship to continue uninterrupted while the new work was erected around it. Only at the last minute was the old work taken down and the two parts of the church united with the least possible interruption to the daily round of the liturgy. In the 1160s, therefore, perhaps between 1163 and 1167, the Crusaders completed their choir, ambulatory, and transepts. For the first time all the most holy sites had been brought within a single structure, and so they remain today.

This analysis of the structural history of the Crusader Church of the Holy Sepulchre

Lying directly south of the rock of Calvary is the 11th station of the Cross, the Latin chapel of the Nailing to the Cross. The ceiling of the chapel is decorated with mosaics, one of which has survived from the Crusader period. On the back wall is a modern mosaic depicting the nailing of Jesus to the cross, above a 16th-century silvered bronze altar donated by Ferdinand I de' Medici. To the left can be seen the 13th station of the Cross, known as Our Lady of the Sorrows or Stabat Mater, commemorating the sadness of Mary on removing the body of Jesus from the cross.

provides a context for the Crusaders' work on the Edicule. The accounts by John of Würzburg ca.1170 and by Theoderic before 1174 show that the Edicule had by then reached its fullest development. The Chapel of the Angel was solidly walled on three sides as it is today but then still had three doorways. The interior of both the tomb chamber and the Chapel of the Angel were covered with mosaics and other ornamentation, and there were at least fourteen Latin inscriptions around the exterior, in the Chapel of the Angel and in the tomb chamber, and around the ironwork screens enclosing the parochial altar built against the west end of the Edicule.

How much earlier the Edicule had reached this form we do not know, but it seems probable that the Crusaders' first significant works in the Church of the Holy Sepulchre were concentrated on the two holiest sites, Calvary and the tomb. Only when these were completed was attention turned to the much greater task of the choir and transepts. If this is true, the Edicule would have been embellished at about the same time that the works of Calvary were in progress, that is to say in the 1140s.

In the middle of the century the Byzantine emperor Manuel I Comnenos (1143–80) covered the burial shelf in the tomb with gold. With the roof of the Edicule now covered with plates of gilded bronze, the cupola sheeted with plates of gilded silver and topped by a gilded cross on which stood a gilded dove (which had replaced the silver figure of Christ), the decoration of the Edicule had reached a peak of magnificence it has never since regained.

In the autumn of 1187, following the defeat of the Kingdom of Jerusalem at the battle of the Horns of Hattin, the silver on the exterior of the Edicule was stripped off and minted into coins to pay the knights and sergeants defending the city, the new coins bearing a representation of the Holy Sepulchre they were paid to defend. Jerusalem surrendered to Saladin on 2 October 1187. None of the buildings were looted. The Church of the Resurrection was closed for three days while its future was discussed. In the end it was decided to follow the example of Caliph 'Umar who on his capture of the city in 638 had confirmed the Christians in their possession of the church. It was not therefore demolished as some had advised, but left in the hands of the Eastern Christians from whom the Crusaders had seized it eighty-eight years before. Four Syrian priests were permitted to remain in the church.

The Centuries of Decay
A.D. 1187–1555

For the next few years the church and the vast priory must have been all but deserted, and it may have been at this time that all the doors but one were walled up. During Crusader times and perhaps much earlier one entrance was from the west, through the Gate of St. Mary, a decorated Crusader arch that is still to be seen on Christian Quarter Street at its junction with Greek Orthodox Patriarchate Street.

This route led down by thirty steps to the Rotunda of the Anastasis, where its lower steps can still be seen immediately west of the Latin chapel of St. Mary Magdalene and the Franciscan choir. It was perhaps also at this time that the eastern of the two great doors leading to the church from the Parvis was closed, and perhaps also the north and south doors of the Edicule, previously used by pilgrims entering and leaving the Tomb of Christ.

In the two years following the fall of Jerusalem in 1187, more than fifty castles fell to Saladin and the greater part of the Kingdom of Jerusalem including Acre, but Tyre held out. Pope Gregory VIII called for a new crusade as early as 29 October 1187. In November Richard of Poitou, later King Richard of England, was the first ruler north of the Alps to take the cross, and in July 1190 he and King Philip II of France set out from Vézelay in Burgundy, arriving at Acre in the summer of 1191. Within a month Acre had been recaptured by this Third Crusade. King Richard then advanced down the coast, taking Jaffa and twice during the next few months advancing within a few miles, indeed on one occasion to within sight, of Jerusalem. In September 1192 a truce was arranged allowing the Crusaders to retain control of the coast between Acre and Jaffa.

Under this treaty Christian pilgrims were to be free to go up to Jerusalem. Hubert Walter, bishop of Salisbury, who led the third group to go that autumn, requested of Saladin

> that at the Tomb of the Lord, which he had visited and where the divine rites were only occasionally celebrated in the barbarous manner of the Syrians, the sacred liturgy be permitted to be celebrated somewhat more becomingly by two Latin priests and the same number of deacons, together with the Syrians, and that they be supported by the offerings of pilgrims.

Saladin agreed and the bishop appointed the priests and deacons. But when a little later an embassy from the Byzantine emperor Isaac Angelus asked that control of the Holy Sepulchre should revert to the Orthodox church, Saladin refused. No one sect would be allowed to dominate, and — as the well-known Crusader historian Runciman stated — "like the Ottoman Sultans after him, he would be arbiter of them all."

Saladin's successors were not so tolerant; pilgrims found themselves required to pay considerable fees. By 1217 Thietmar found the church "without lamps, without honour,

A closed entrance to the Holy Sepulchre. Following the capture of Jerusalem by Saladin on 2 October 1187, the doors of the Holy Sepulchre were sealed for three days and subsequently one of the two great twin doors was walled up, remaining so till today.

without reverence, and always shut unless opened to pilgrims on payment of fees." But in 1229 the Crusaders recovered Jerusalem for ten years under the terms of a treaty between the German emperor Frederick II of Hohenstaufen and the sultan al-Kamil. On 17 March Frederick entered the city. The next day, a Sunday, he went to attend Mass in the Church of the Holy Sepulchre, but not a single priest was there. Frederick placed a royal crown on the altar of Calvary, and then crowned himself king of Jerusalem.

Within weeks Frederick had left the kingdom amid a chorus of disapproval at his self-coronation and his policies. The Crusaders' hold on Jerusalem was never strong during the years that followed. After the expiration of the treaty in 1239, the city remained uneasily in their hands until the summer of 1244, when ten thousand Khwarizmian Turkish horsemen swept down from the northwest, and broke into Jerusalem on 11 July. The citadel held out until surrendered under an agreement of safe conduct on 23 August, the terms of which were broken. No mercy was shown. The Khwarizmians entered the Church of the Holy Sepulchre, broke open the tombs of the kings, slaughtered the Christians who had taken refuge in front of the Edicule, and decapitated the priests who were celebrating at the altars.

In November Robert, patriarch of Jerusalem, the bishops of the kingdom, the vice-master of the Temple, the prior of the Holy Sepulchre, and others wrote from Acre to the prelates of France and England describing what had happened:

laying sacrilegious hands on the tomb of the Lord's resurrection, they defiled it in many ways, overturning from its base the marble cladding placed around it. . . . The carved columns placed in front of the tomb of the Lord for decoration they removed, sending them as a sign of victory to the tomb of the evil Mohammed, to the disgrace of the Christians.

These events, formally recorded by those in the best position to know the facts, may have been exaggerated from the despair of the moment and the need to rouse sympathy in Europe. But the details of the damage done to the Edicule are precise. They also go far to explain the condition of the Edicule as it is first visible to us in drawings made by pilgrims during the following centuries, constructed of blocks that seem stripped of any proper covering.

Italian pilgrims at the entrance of the Church of the Holy Sepulchre. A 15th-century edition of Marco Polo's Book of Marvels.

During these difficult years from 1192 and onwards through the thirteenth century, pilgrimage to Jerusalem, to the place of Christ's death and resurrection, still continued. In Jerusalem itself a new force — the Franciscan order — was emerging to protect as far as was possible the Holy Places and to care for pilgrims. At their General Chapter in 1217, St. Francis of Assisi and the assembled friars divided the world into distinct Franciscan provinces, the most important of which was the Province of the Holy Land. St. Francis himself, in the course of a long visit to Egypt, Syria, and Palestine in 1219–20, established contacts with the Muslim authorities and created settlements of friars designed to ensue the continuity of liturgical functions in the Holy Places. After 1291 the friars had to retreat to Cyprus, but from 1322 onwards they were present in the Church of the Holy Sepulchre and in 1328 Pope John XXII gave permission for two friars to be sent to Jerusalem every year. By 1335 the Franciscans had established a monastery on Mount Sion, where they remained until expelled in 1551, finally moving to their present convent at St. Saviour's in 1560.

Since the early fourteenth century, the Franciscans have provided in Jerusalem for the reception and care of pilgrims, whose numbers seem to have increased enormously. The "Spring Voyage" from Venice brought the pilgrims to Jaffa, whence under conditions often of great difficulty they made their way to and from Jerusalem, and sometimes even as far as Mount Sinai. Subject to robbery and to demands for payments of every kind, their stay in Palestine, usually of no more than five or six weeks, was hazardous but successfully completed by the majority. The accounts they wrote, sometimes individual but often based on pilgrim guide books many times reissued, at first in manuscript but by the end of the fifteenth century in print, are almost the only source we have for what it was like to be a pilgrim and for the state of the places they went to see. Some of these pilgrimages were very large, led by the greatest nobles of their time. Others were undertaken by confraternities,

Ordination of a knight of the Holy Sepulcher in the Church of the Holy Sepulcher in Jerusalem by the Guardian of the Franciscans. Illustration from the Itinerary of Heinrich Wölffli—1520.

like the Knightly Brotherhood of the Holy Land in Haarlem, of whose thirteen members the artist Jan van Scorel, who accompanied them in 1520, made a notable painting. Not all came from the West. Many came from the East, including many from Russia. For all, the goal of their pilgrimage was Christ's tomb.

When they went home some of these pilgrims erected large-scale copies of the tomb to serve as a focus for their celebration of Easter in future years, and some even undertook the construction of a "New Jerusalem," a series of chapels and shrines where the whole drama of Easter could be followed from place to place during Easter Week. One such was in the town of Görlitz on the Neisse River on the far eastern borders of Germany, created in the last years of the fifteenth and the first years of the sixteenth century. Of about the same date was the "Nuova Gerusalemme" at San Vivaldo in Valdelsa in the Tuscan woods near Florence where in the first decade of the sixteenth century Fra Tommaso da Firenze erected twenty-four separate chapels to bring Jerusalem to life for those who would never have the opportunity to go there.

From what these pilgrims wrote and even more from the drawings a very few of them made, or had made by servants travelling with them, we can see that the Edicule seems to have been in continuous decay. Although the Franciscans had secured sole rights in the tomb before the middle of the fourteenth century, they did not recover the keys of the Edicule from the Muslims for another hundred years. There is no record of any major repairs, perhaps because they were forbidden, but at some date in the early fifteenth century the Franciscans seem to have been able to make alterations to the tomb chamber that made it more convenient for the celebration of the mass. Previously they had used a removable wooden altar placed on the marble slab over the burial couch, as they do again today. Now they probably replaced the marble sheets covering the front of the tomb,

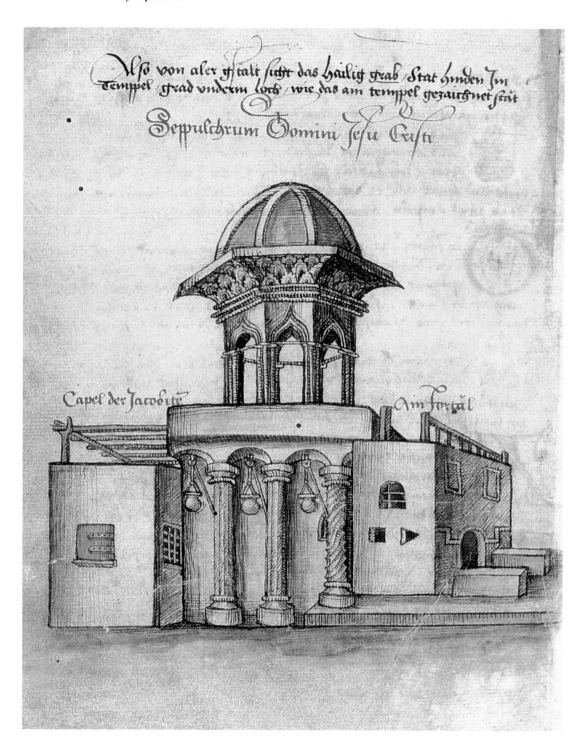

Also von aler gstalt sicht das hailig grab Stat hinden Im tempel grad underm loch / wie das am tempel gezaichnet stat

Sepulchrum Domini Jesu Cristi

Capel der Jacobite

Am fortäl

concealing the three circular openings through which from at least the early twelfth century pilgrims had been able to see, touch, and perhaps kiss the actual rock of the burial shelf on which the body of Christ had lain. The rock of the burial couch has been completely hidden ever since. The marble slab over the burial couch the Franciscans did not change. Already in 1345 an anonymous English pilgrim had described the slab, which had "lips on the sides, and in the middle of the slab there was cut a streak," exactly as it remains today, 650 years later.

The Parvis or forecourt of the Church of the Holy Sepulchre is known to us from drawings that date back to the fourteenth century. The cupola over the round church of the Anastasis was then still in the form of the open cone first erected in the early ninth century, although rebuilt after the destruction of 1009. The Crusader campanile still had five stories. But otherwise everything was very much as it can be seen today.

Colored ink drawing of the Edicule, made in 1487, presumably from sketches taken by Konrad von Grunenberg during his visit to the church.

Repairs and Division of the Church
A.D. 1517–1808

During the fourteenth and fifteenth centuries under the Mamluks generally good relations with the West and with Byzantium had encouraged the flow of pilgrims, especially in the second half of the period. Conditions changed early in the sixteenth century, partly as a result of the Reformation, which led to a decrease in pilgrimage from large parts of Europe north of the Alps, but also as a result of the conquest of Syria by the Ottoman Turks in 1517. For the next four centuries Jerusalem was the seat of an unimportant district of the pashalik of Damascus. Heavy taxation, poor administration, and arbitrary justice took their toll on the Christian communities, and by the beginning of the nineteenth century the city and its buildings were in a neglected state.

For the Franciscans problems had begun soon after the Turkish conquest. In 1552, after several attempts, Sulayman the Magnificent (1520–66) finally expelled the friars from their monastery on Mount Sion, but almost immediately afterwards Boniface of Ragusa arrived to take up the office of Custos of the Holy Land. During the eight years of his first custody (he was Custos again in 1564–65), Boniface not only secured a new site for the convent but also undertook the restoration of several of the Holy Places including, in the Church of the Holy Sepulchre, the Stone of Unction and the Edicule.

The Edicule was in a state of collapse in 1555 when Pope Julius III (1550–55), urged on by the Holy Roman Emperor, Charles V, and his son King Philip of Spain, instructed Boniface to undertake its restoration, for which imperial funds were to be made available. Boniface opened the tomb on 27 August 1555, describing later in a solemn letter how he had to take the structure down to the ground so that the rebuilt fabric should rise stronger and last longer.

> The demolition brought forth clearly to our very eyes the sepulchre of the Lord Most Holy cut out of the rock. . . . When we had to remove one of the alabaster slabs covering the Sepulchre, [one of those] on which the holy mystery of the Mass is celebrated, there appeared laid open to us that ineffable place on which the Son of Man lay for three days.

In a book written later for King Philip, who had been given the empty title of King of Jerusalem by his father on his marriage to Queen Mary of England in 1553, and who had eventually paid for the restoration of the Edicule, Boniface described how he had "restored that holy place from the very foundations and decorated it with slabs of shining marble." Engravings of the Edicule made in the next century show that Boniface must have reused much of the old stone for the main structure, but his cupola was entirely new, a work of classical architecture decorated with cupids' heads in the new Renaissance style.

Because Boniface had seen the remains of the original rock-cut tomb within the Edicule, he was also able to draw a parallel with a tomb he had seen south of the city in the great

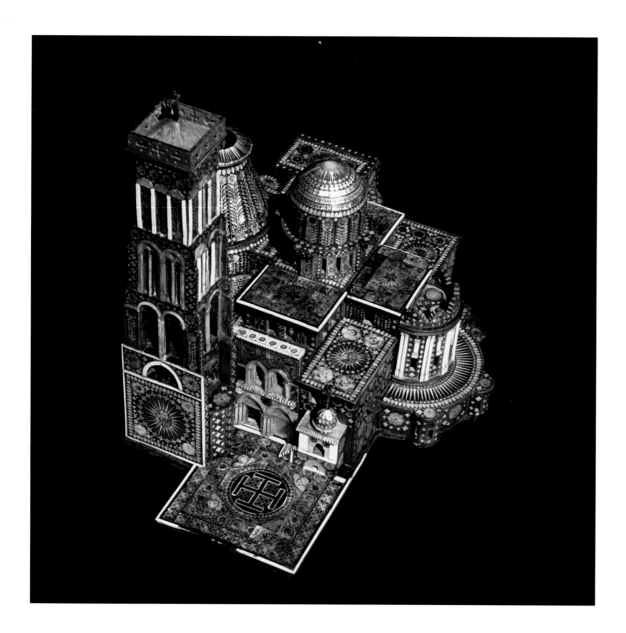

cemetery of rock-cut tombs at Akeldama, on the southern slopes of the Valley of Hinnom:

> I found there a tomb similar in every way to that in which Christ's body lay. I pointed this out to the [Franciscan] brothers that they might rejoice and show it to their successors and to pilgrims coming to the Holy Land. I was very well able to know this, for I saw the place of the Lord's body . . . when I restored that holy place.

The original rock-cut burial shelf of Christ had been covered up again in completing the restoration of the Edicule, but Boniface was able to point to the tomb in Akeldama as the best way of understanding what Christ's burial place had originally looked like. Sadly this tomb in Akeldama cannot be identified today, and Boniface remains, four hundred and fifty years later, the last person to have seen the burial place of Christ in its entirety.

Despite Boniface's efforts, pilgrimage at this time was fraught with danger. When Melchior von Seydlitz and his companions from Görlitz were in Jerusalem in 1557, they were arrested by the governor, sent in chains on foot to Damascus, to Aleppo, and finally to Constantinople where they spent two years breaking stone before finally being released.

The centuries of Turkish rule were not easy for any of the communities. Although to some extent protected under the milet system, whereby the Greek Orthodox patriarch in Constantinople was responsible throughout Ottoman lands not only for the religious but also

Model of the Church of the Holy Sepulchre, 17th-18th century, Musée de la Société des Antiquaires de l'Ouest, Poitiers. Such models made from olive wood and inlaid with mother of pearl, ivory, or bone were probably made for pilgrims in workshops in the Jerusalem area. The roof of the model can be lifted, revealing the Edicule and the interior decoration.

An engraving of 1698 by Cornelius de Bruyn provides a view of the interior of the Rotunda and the Edicule as it existed at the end of the Middle Ages.
This engraving was reproduced in many books during the 17th and the 18th centuries.

the secular affairs of his people, the Orthodox in Jerusalem were as much subject to the vagaries of Turkish rule and taxes as were the other communities. The Latins, enjoying the protection of the Catholic rulers of Europe and the watchful eye of Venice, were also reasonably secure, although subject to arbitrary intervention.

Relations between the communities worsened during the seventeenth century, especially after 1633, when first one and then another community — Greek, Latin, or Armenian — succeeded in obtaining and then in losing control over one part or another of the Church of the Holy Sepulchre. It was in this situation in 1662 that the Orthodox patriarch Dositheos founded the Greek Confraternity of the Holy Sepulchre that ever since has occupied the great complex of monastic buildings east of the Parvis.

By this time the Armenians had established their presence in the gallery on the south side of the Rotunda of the Anastasis, and from time to time asserted their rights in other parts of the building.

The situation was complicated by the seemingly unending war between the Ottoman empire and the Venetian republic on the one hand, and by conflict with Austria and Poland on the other, at a time when the influence of France and Spain was on the wane. Inevitably this state of affairs weakened the position of the Latin community. There was moreover an urgent necessity to undertake restorations and repairs. After thirty years of negotiation the Latins were at last able in 1719 to obtain agreement from the Sublime Porte (the Ottoman

department of foreign affairs) allowing them to rebuild the dome over the Rotunda of the Anastasis. This they then reconstructed for the last time as an open cone, a form it had first been given in the ninth century.

The growing interest of Russia in the Church of the Holy Sepulchre is most remarkably shown in the pilgrimage of Arsenii Sukhanov in 1651 – 53. Although firmly defending the purity of Russian Orthodoxy, he was happy to take back to Russia one of the olive wood, mother-of-pearl, and bone or ivory models of the Church that had been produced in Bethlehem since about 1600 for sale to pilgrims. It was on the basis of this model that the Russian patriarch Nikon (d. 1681) had a full-scale copy of the entire Church of the Holy Sepulchre built at Novoierusalimsky Monastyr, near Istra, some 80 kilometers (50 miles) east of Moscow.

The question of the Holy Places had now become one of the great issues of European diplomacy. In treaty after treaty with Turkey during the eighteenth century articles were inserted to secure the liberty of the Catholic or Orthodox religion in the territory of the Ottoman empire. The first tentative steps were now taken to codify the existing situation, the Status Quo, as a basis for a lasting settlement, but when agreement was reached — as in 1740 between France and Turkey or at Kuchuk-Kainardji in 1774, when Russia sought to secure the right to make representations on behalf of the Orthodox church — it was broken some years later.

By now the outside world was beginning to make itself more directly felt. A new type of Western visitor, the scientific or literary traveler, sometimes accompanied by an artist, was appearing alongside the by now somewhat restricted flow of Western pilgrims. By contrast, Eastern pilgrimage was on the increase, to judge by the printed guidebooks now available.

The French Revolution, with its proscription of religion, Napoleon's Egyptian expedition in 1797 and his invasion, short-lived and abortive, of Palestine, and the ensuing long years of war involving both the Western and Eastern powers, first involved and then distanced the interests of the Western powers from Turkey and the Ottoman question. Slowly but surely, the Orthodox church consolidated its position in the Church of the Holy Sepulchre and in the Holy Places in general. The position of the Latin community was correspondingly weakened by the distraction of the Western powers.

A group of eastern Christian pilgrims pray in the Chapel of the Angel. In the background a priest kneels in devotion in front of the Sepulchre, while two kavass *guard the entrance to the tomb. Luigi Mayer, 1801.*

Fire, Rebuilding and the Last Century of Ottoman Rule
A.D. 1808–1917

Sailors from the French fleet, visiting the Holy Land, walk in ceremonial procession around the reconstructed Edicule and Rotunda, rebuilt as a consequence of the 1808 fire. Colored engraving of E.F. Paris, 1862.

On 12 October 1808 (30 September by the Julian calendar), fire broke out in the southern gallery of the Anastasis. The flames spread quickly to the northern gallery and up to the conical roof erected only ninety years before. After five hours the great beams came crashing to the floor, destroying the cupola of the Edicule. The fire scorched the columns and piers of the Rotunda and the walls of the Edicule, but was stopped by its door. The door survived the fire and is preserved today in the Museum of the Greek Orthodox patriarchate. Blackened and slightly charred near the bottom on the outside but otherwise intact, the door seems to have protected the interior of the Edicule from the worst effects of the heat and smoke, although half the velvet hangings in the Chapel of the Angel were scorched.

Meanwhile the fire had spread rapidly north to the Muslim dwellings over the Latin apartments north of the Anastasis. These caught fire and fell into some of the Latin rooms below. To the east, the fire spread to the roof of the Greek Katholikon, the Crusader choir, and reached as far as its eastern apse. To the south, the Greek apartments were burned out, together with the chapels of Calvary.

The Latin, Greek, and Armenian communities all sought some share in the rebuilding, but the Western powers were distracted by the Napoleonic wars. It was thus the Greek Orthodox community, relying on an Ottoman decree of 1757, that in March 1809 obtained from Sultan Mahmud II (1809–39) a new *firman* authorizing them to restore the church. The work was completed over the following year under the direction of a Greek architect from Istanbul, Nikolaos Ch. Komnenos (1770–1821).

With the support of the patriarch, Komnenos had volunteered his services for the reconstruction of the Church of the Holy Sepulchre. He left Istanbul on 3 May 1809 and the restored church was consecrated on 11 September 1810, a remarkably short period given the extent of what had to be done. The work was carried out by "Romaic" (i.e., Orthodox) builders from the patriarchate of Jerusalem supervised by Komnenos and Drakon, a master mason from Rhodes, together with Anatolian Greek master masons and plasterers from Cappadocia.

Komnenos and his workforce restored the Katholikon, rebuilding its eastern apse with a distinctive shell-shaped roof, restored the Calvary chapels, and reconstructed the Rotunda. The columns and piers of the Rotunda were cased in plastered rubble, the roof replaced as a proper dome, and the interior completely redecorated. The Edicule itself was rebuilt from the foundations in March 1810, as an inscription on the front records. Only the marble cladding of the tomb chamber and the lowest course of the exterior were left in position. The Chapel of the Angel, the vaults over the chapel and over the tomb chamber, the exterior walls, and the cupola were rebuilt in the Ottoman-Baroque style. A

member of the Greek community, Maximos Simaios, recorded in some detail what he had seen of the original rock-cut burial shelf, partly revealed in the course of the work. He is the last person to have seen it, almost two centuries ago.

The Coptic Chapel attached to the west end of the Edicule was also destroyed in the fire. It was at first omitted in the rebuilding, but had been replaced by 1818, appearing on a plan of the church drawn that year.

Komnenos's work has not been commended by Western critics, yet it saved the building from collapse until a thorough restoration at last became possible in the 1970s. Perhaps his greatest achievement was to rebuild the roof of the Anastasis as a true dome for the first time since the destruction of what may have been Constantine's original dome in the early ninth century. By the 1840s, however, Komnenos's dome was leaking and unstable. Negotiations over its replacement lasted until 1862 when France, Russia, and Turkey agreed to share the cost. The work was carried out in 1867–68, the basis being a prefabricated wrought-iron framework, bolted together on site. When in 1979 this framework was inspected and surveyed it was found to be in perfect condition and constructed with great precision. The model for this remarkable structure is still preserved in the Russian Orthodox Hospice, while the actual frame remains at the heart of the new dome constructed by British engineers in 1979–80.

The reconstruction of 1809–10 by the Greek Orthodox community at a time of Western diplomatic weakness was recognized by a *firman* of 1811 as not intruding on the established rights of the Latin and Armenian communities. One result of this was that the Latins were reinstated in their possession of the Edicule, although the Greeks retained custody of it. The situation in the Church of the Holy Sepulchre as a whole and in the other Holy Places was finally brought to a state of equilibrium by the *firman* of Sultan 'Abd al-Majid I issued in February 1852, which declared that the situation in which, and the conditions under which, the communities at that time stood should be maintained. Certain modifications were made at the time, and there have been some modifications since, but this is the legal basis of the Status Quo, under which the communities in the Holy Places live side by side today. The Status Quo was maintained by the Treaty of Paris in 1855 and by the Treaty of Berlin in 1872, and has been maintained in turn by the

The Greek patriarch seated on his throne officiates over prayer before the Iconostasis of the Katholikon. In the center of the foreground is a small pedestal known as the "compas" marking the traditional center of the world. An engraving from a series produced by David Roberts in 1839.

Ottoman, British Mandate, Jordanian, and Israeli governments to this day.

In 1831 Muhammad 'Ali, pasha of Egypt, invaded Ottoman Syria and occupied Jerusalem. During the next nine years, under the pasha's modernizing rule, public security was improved, the roads made safe, and a flood of western travelers entered the country, among them the English traveler and manuscript-hunter Robert Curzon, then on his tour of the monasteries of the Levant. Curzon was in the Church of the Holy Sepulchre for Orthodox Easter on 3 May 1834, and watched the ceremony of the Holy Fire from the Latin gallery on the north side of the Rotunda, where the Egyptian governor, Ibrahim Pasha, was also seated. The church was perhaps exceptionally crowded and the excitement at fever pitch, but Curzon's description shows that the ceremony went more or less as normal until the departure of Ibrahim Pasha. An immense crush then developed around the Stone of Unction as people literally fought to pass out of the church through the single door into the Parvis. The pasha escaped with difficulty, Curzon barely got away, but more than a hundred died and many more were injured. The pasha, as representative of the Egyptian government then in control of Palestine, took on the immediate task of restoring order and dealing with the dead and wounded.

Among others from the West who were now reaching Palestine in ever increasing numbers were artists, notably David Roberts, and missionaries and scholars, sometimes one and the same, such as the American Protestant Edward Robinson who arrived in 1838. Robinson, as enthusiastic to authenticate the Scriptures as he was to repudiate almost every shrine in Jerusalem, rapidly decided that the Holy Sepulchre, which he visited only once, was a "pious superstition." This was the more unfortunate because Robinson was already an outstanding bible scholar and since 1837 professor of biblical literature at the Union Theological Seminary in New York. Robinson made many remarkable discoveries and observations in Palestine, not least in Jerusalem where he was the first properly to explore the tunnel between the Gihon spring and the Pool of Siloam, and where Robinson's Arch at the southwest corner of the Temple Mount still bears his name. But his authority undoubtedly gave weight to the rejection of the authenticity of the Holy Sepulchre by some Protestant groups and thus to the search for an alternative location. This was to lead General Gordon in 1883 on the morning after his arrival in Jerusalem to

"discover" a new Calvary outside the north wall of the city. A tomb nearby was subsequently identified as the Tomb of Christ, now known as the Garden Tomb, and preserved as a beautiful place of prayer for Christian pilgrims. However, most scholars agree that this in fact could not be the place where Christ was buried.

In the years since, the heated debates surrounding claims such as Robinson's and Gordon's have died down, and there has been little controversy about the authenticity of the site in serious academic discussion during the twentieth century. Increasing knowledge of the topography and archaeology of the northwestern quarter of Jerusalem and of the site of the Holy Sepulchre church in particular, although still very inadequate both in content and quality, has raised no serious obstacle to acceptance of the authenticity of the site.

There was much sound scholarship on Jerusalem in the nineteenth century, most remarkably *The Architectural History of the Church of the Holy Sepulchre* published in 1849 by the Englishman Robert Willis, Jacksonian Professor of Mechanical Engineering at the University of Cambridge. For the very first time the structural history of the tomb and the church were described in detail, using a measured survey — the first — by the architect J.J. Scoles, wooden models of the church made for pilgrims preserved in the British Museum, and a series of new Russian lithographs and other drawings. It is only as one reads carefully through Willis's book that the realization dawns that he had never visited Jerusalem. Yet his study is a landmark in the history of the church and still of use today.

Willis wrote without the benefit even of photographs, although the first had already been taken in Jerusalem in 1839, ten years before his book was published. The earliest

The present appearance of the facade of the Church of the Holy Sepulchre is almost identical to that shown in this engraving by W. H. Bartlett from 1842. Note the missing upper floors of the bell tower to the left, destroyed by an earthquake and repaired to the present height in 1719.

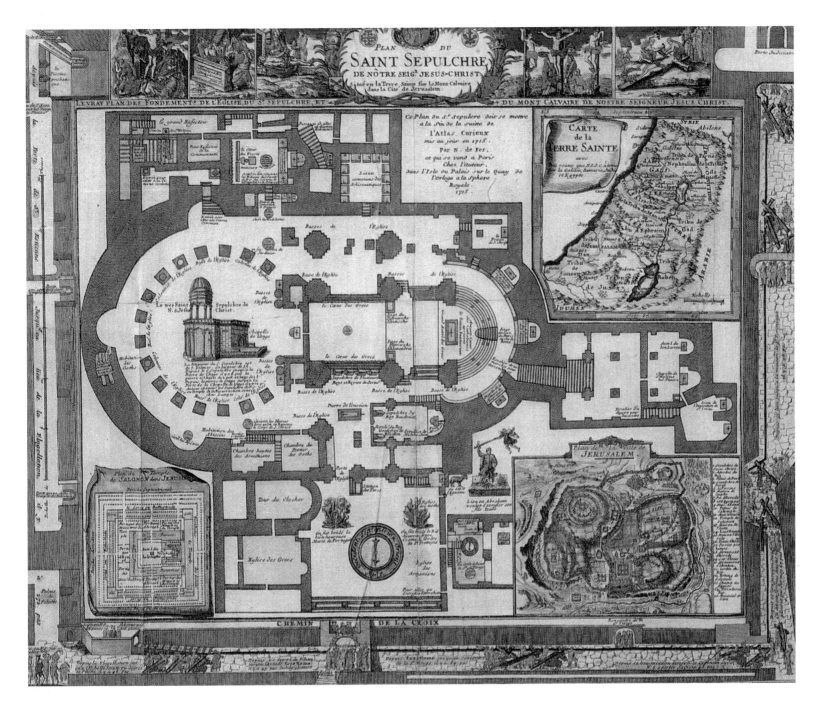

The first known detailed plan of the Church of the Holy Sepulchre, produced by De Fer in 1715. The plan is bordered by scenes of the 14 Stations of the Cross along the Via Dolorosa and within the church. In three corners are maps of the Holy Land, Jerusalem, and a plan of Solomon's Temple.

photographs of the outside of the Church of the Holy Sepulchre were taken in 1850 by the Frenchman Maxime du Camp, the work of the German Auguste Salzmann followed in 1854, and the tide became a flood. Perhaps the most remarkable photograph was taken in 1861 looking north across the Muristan towards the church: the Muristan is an open field and the church looks as if it were in the countryside rather than in the middle of the Old City. It was to be some years before photographs were taken inside the church.

The last years of the nineteenth and the first of the twentieth century were a relatively peaceful time for the Church of the Holy Sepulchre. Most striking was the growth in pilgrimage from Orthodox Russia. By the beginning of the new century pilgrims were coming every Easter to Jerusalem, intent on taking home with them candles lit by the Holy Fire. Easter 1914 was the last of the era, however, to see the Russians in Jerusalem. By 1915 Russia and Turkey were on opposite sides in the First World War, and the revolution two years later brought an end to Russian involvement with the Holy Land for the next seventy years.

The Church of the Holy Sepulchre in the Twentieth Century A.D. 1917–2000

Ottoman rule over Jerusalem came to an end on 9 December 1917 when the mayor surrendered the city to British and Australian forces under the command of General Sir Edmund Allenby. Two days later, after entering the city on foot through Jaffa Gate, Allenby spoke from the steps of the Citadel to "the inhabitants of Jerusalem the Blessed":

> since your city is regarded with affection by adherents of three of the great religions of mankind, and its soil has been consecrated by the prayers and pilgrimages of multitudes of devout people of these three religions for many centuries, therefore do I make known to you that every sacred building, monument, holy spot, shrine, traditional site, endowment, pious bequest, or customary place of prayer, of whatsoever form of the three religions, will be maintained and protected according to the existing customs and beliefs of those to whose faiths they are sacred.

The text of Allenby's speech had been forwarded by the British government, which thus declared its duty to the Holy Places and, in the case of the Christian sites, to the upholding of the Status Quo, as had the Ottomans before, and as its successors, Jordanian and Israeli, were later to do.

In the area they referred to as Occupied Enemy Territory Administration (OETA), the British appointed an Inspector of Antiquities almost immediately upon their arrival. They were soon alarmed by the state of the Holy Sepulchre. In a long report on the antiquities of Jerusalem and its district written late in 1919, Captain E. Mackay, Inspector of Antiquities, OETA (South), found that the Edicule was in imminent danger of falling.

Ronald Storrs, the military governor of Jerusalem, at once requested the Latin, Greek, and Armenian patriarchs to suspend the custom of hanging Lenten ornaments on the tomb, as they were accustomed to do under the Status Quo. Two of the patriarchs agreed, but the third could not, and Storrs transmitted his intention to lay responsibility "for any possible damage accruing to the sacred structure . . . at the door" of the third patriarch.

Until the dome was rebuilt in 1868 and the central opening provided with a cover, rain had poured down through the eye of the dome on to the Edicule, rotting the iron cramps holding the stones together. In 1926, alarmed by the open joints between the bulging stones, the by-then Mandate government of Palestine carried out a survey of the tomb. After lengthy negotiations, the agreement of the religious communities was obtained for the removal of some stones on the north side of the Edicule to allow inspection of the core of the wall. The British were somewhat reassured. Their report revealed that there was an inner structure that seemed vertical and sound enough.

The church as a whole, already in parlous state from years of structural neglect and inadequate maintenance, was severely damaged in the great earthquake of 1927, but

Following the 1927 earthquake the structure of the Edicule became unstable. In 1946 it was decided by the Public Works Department of the British mandatory Government to surround the Edicule with scaffoldings. The girders have remained there ever since.

the Edicule held fast. The most urgent work, the reconstruction of the dome over the crossing of the Katholikon, was completed for the Greek Orthodox community in 1935 to the design of the British architect William Harvey. The building was propped up with steel and timber shores, and for the next thirty years the whole church was a forest of scaffolding. In 1946 a further survey of the Edicule showed that its "condition must be on the border of instability and reconstruction cannot be safely neglected." In March 1947, as the last of the Mandate government's works in the Church of the Holy Sepulchre, the Public Works Department wrapped the Edicule in a cradle of steel.

So great was the despair of those years that the Latin community put forward a plan for rebuilding the Church of the Holy Sepulchre to a completely new design. The work of the architects Luigi Marangoni and Antonio Barluzzi, commissioned in 1939 and intended originally to be displayed at the abortive Esposizione Universale at Rome in 1942, the scheme would have seen the complete removal of the ancient church and the creation of a vast building in the center of an open plaza rivaling in scale the Temple Mount, the Haram esh Sherif. Eventually published in 1949, on the eighth centenary of the consecration of the Crusader church in 1149, the scheme found little support and was never seriously considered.

As an outcome of the 1948 Arab-Israeli war, the care of the Holy Places, including the Church of the Holy Sepulchre, passed to the Jordanian government, which maintained the tradition of the Turkish and British administrations in protecting and upholding the Status Quo. By now, too, in an improved ecumenical climate, restoration had become possible. A Common Technical Bureau, set up in 1958 by the three great communities, achieved a brilliant recovering of the ancient fabric — Constantinian, Byzantine, Crusader — involving the Katholikon, the transepts, and the Rotunda.

Hostilities renewed, and following the 1967 war the government of Israel took on the mantle of all previous administrations in protecting the Holy Places of Jerusalem and maintaining the Status Quo. The long work of restoration in the Church of the Holy Sepulchre continued uninterruptedly. Above the Tomb of Christ a new dome crowning the Rotunda of the Anastasis was constructed in 1979-81 by British engineers for the Latin, Greek Orthodox, and Armenian communities following the outline of the wrought iron frame of 1868 which was left in position inside the new inner and outer shells. The interior of the new dome remained scaffolded and undecorated for many years, but agreement was eventually reached between the communities and the present decoration completed in 1996 in time for an ecumenical ceremony on 2 January 1997 marking the beginning of the triennium of preparation for the Great Jubilee of the Year 2000. Meanwhile in 1988 Professor George Lavas, architect to the Greek Orthodox community, had successfully completed the restoration of Golgotha, revealing and displaying the top of the Rock of Calvary for all to see.

Today, the Church of the Holy Sepulchre faces the third millennium with great expectations. Increasing numbers of pilgrims and visitors are predicted, and future restoration and conservation plans are being presented to improve the physical condition of the church as the most important Christian site in the Holy Land.

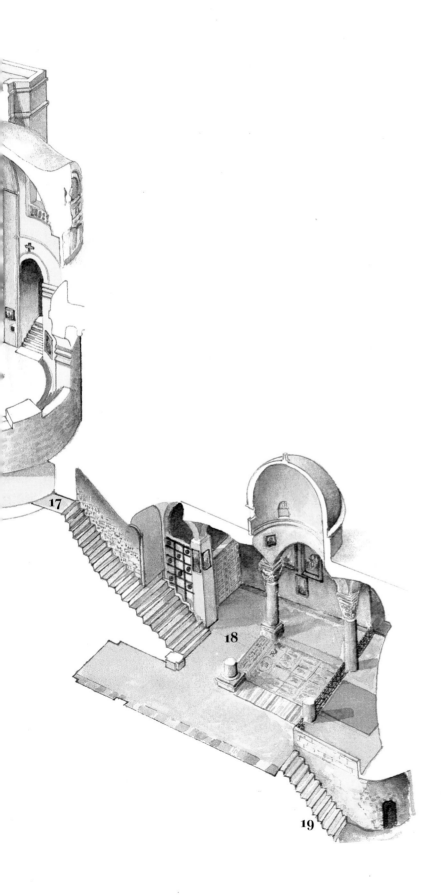

17

18

19

SECTION OF THE CHURCH
OF THE HOLY SEPULCHRE:

1. *Parvis or entrance courtyard*
2. *Chapel of St. James the Less*
3. *Chapel of St. John the Baptist*
4. *Chapel of the Forty Martyrs*
5. *Chapel of the Agony of the Virgin*
6. *Chapel of Adam*
7. *Rock of Golgotha*
8. *Greek Chapel of Golgotha*
9. *Stone of Unction*
10. *Chapel of the Angel*
11. *Christ's Tomb*
12. *Rotunda*
13. *Chapel of St. Mary the Egyptian*
14. *The center of the world, the "compas"*
15. *Katholikon*
16. *Arches of the Virgin*
17. *Stairs to the crypt of St. Helena*
18. *Chapel of St. Helena*
19. *To the Chapel of the Invention of the Holy Cross*

The Art of the Crusader Church of the Holy Sepulchre

The Crusader Church of the Holy Sepulchre was one of the most magnificent pilgrimage and tomb churches in the Christian world, distinct from any contemporary counterpart. The church stood out with its sophisticated architectural design and its luxurious decorations, blending Eastern and Western inspirations, and had a significant impact on art in the Crusader States in the mid-twelfth century. The work was carried out by masons, architects, sculptors, mosaicists, and painters of different origins working in various styles, creating a visual cosmopolitan expression. At the core a Western pilgrimage-type church with an apse, an ambulatory and three radiating chapels, the church incorporated Eastern elements — the two domes on high drums and the focus on the domed crossing and the Rotunda — that granted it its special character. Other unique elements included the ribbed vaulting, paired columns and half-columns, and broad pointed arches. The rich decoration, most of it lost, consisted of monumental paintings — wall and floor mosaics and frescoes, and decorative and figurative sculpture. The decorative program was centered around the various holy sites within the church, linking the different parts through narrative sequencing. Mentioned by twelfth-century pilgrims were marble floors, doors, altars, bells, grills, icons, textiles, lamps, candlesticks, chalices, croziers, gemellions, enamelwork, metalwork, and goldsmiths' work.

Opposite: the double portal and paired fenestration of the south transept facade.
Above: the central capitals of the lower story of the south transept facade.

The South Transept Facade

The monumental south transept facade, which served as the main entrance to the Crusader Church of the Holy Sepulchre, is one of the richest and most significant manifestations of Crusader art in the Latin Kingdom of Jerusalem. Its original plan included a two-storied double portal, and paired fenestration with broad pointed arches over the doors. These were adorned with figurative and foliate sculpture. Flanking the portals are the exterior domed Chapel of the Franks, and a massive bell tower originally five stories high, to the west.

The double portal with its broad pointed arches was adorned with marble columns and half columns raised on bases and surmounted by capitals. A floral frieze framed the doors and continued horizontally along the wall. It was bounded by sculptured borders: a "bead-and-reel" pattern below, and an "egg-and-dart" design above. Two sculptured lintels were set above the doors. Figural mosaics, no longer extant, occupied the portal tympana (see "Mosaics and Frescoes"). A godroon frieze surrounded the portal-arches and a rosette frieze followed their curves and continued along the wall. The basic motif of this latter frieze is a rosette spiraling around a smaller inner flower. The rosettes, arranged in symmetrical groups of four, are interspersed with small palmettes.

The Figurative Lintel. First scene on the left: **The Raising of Lazarus**. *Second scene from the left:* **Jesus and His Disciples Meet Mary Magdalene and Martha** *(see next pages). Third scene from the left, lower representation:* **The Preparation of the Paschal Lamb**. *Two men, perhaps the disciples Peter and John, prepare the Paschal Lamb under a seven-lobed arch (Luke 22:7–13). An attempt has been made to interpret this scene, together with the two following scenes, as the Expulsion of the Money Changers and the Cleansing of the Temple (Matthew 21:12–14; Mark 11:15–17; Luke 19:45–46; John 2:13–16). Accordingly, the two men surrounded with birds (perhaps doves) would be* traders sitting in the Temple courtyard, which is represented by a seven-lobed arch.

Third scene from the left, upper representation: **Preparations for the Coming Events**. *Under a double arch stands Jesus, a crossed halo about his head, on the left, and a disciple on the right, both watching as another disciple leaves through a doorway to make arrangements for the coming events:* **The Entry to Jerusalem** *and* **The Last Supper** *(depicted in the fourth and fifth scenes). In keeping with the Expulsion of the Money Changers interpretation (see above), Jesus, on the left, is pushing two traders away from the Temple, which is represented by a double arch.*

Above, in the upper story, the pair of windows with pointed arches was similarly decorated with columns, capitals, and friezes. The window-arches were surrounded by an inner godroon frieze and an outer floral frieze depicting leaves intertwined with vine scrolls, which continued horizontally along the wall.

The south transept facade incorporated iconographical and stylistic elements and influences from East and West. The multi-storied facade displays twelve-century French and Spanish influences, whereas the double portal and the pointed arches, the capitals and the friezes — all exhibit affinities with architectural ornaments of the Syro-Palestine region in the sixth to eight centuries.

The Sculptured Lintels of the South Transept Facade

The elaborate decorative plan of the facade included two sculptured lintels adorning the double doors. These lintels are two of the most important artistic remnants of the Latin Kingdom and among the few figurative sculptured works in Crusader Jerusalem.

*Fourth scene from the left: **Bringing the Ass and the Colt**. Two disciples bring the ass and the colt from Bethphage (Matthew 21:1–7; Mark 11:1–7; Luke 19:29–35). In accordance with the Expulsion of the Money Changers interpretation (see above), a bull and a calf represent the cattle bought and sold in the Temple courtyard. Some of the traders, on the right, are watching the occurrences.*

*Fifth scene from the left; heavily damaged: **The Entry to Jerusalem**. Jesus and his disciples enter into Jerusalem, with the Mount of Olives behind them. On the right is the city gate and a palm tree with a crowd around it and children climbing it,*

probably all there to greet Jesus (Matthew 21:8–11; Mark 11:8–11; Luke 19:36–38; John 12:12–19).

*Sixth scene from the left: **The Last Supper**. In the center, under a triple-arched and domed structure (similar to the one in the first scene on the left), is Jesus with a crossed halo about his head. On both his sides are the disciples. Jesus is embracing one of them, probably John. Judas Iscariot is seated on the opposite side of the table. The table is represented by a tablecloth stretched over the sitters' laps, and on it are bread loaves and knives (Matthew 26:20–29; Mark 14:17–25; Luke 22:14–38; John 13:1ff.).*

The lintels were carved on separate thin rectangular marble plaques and added to the portals. There is no consensus as to the time they were completed; some scholars suggest the early 1150s, others arrive at a date later in the twelfth century, before 1187. The lintels were taken down in 1929 for conservation treatment and have been on display ever since in the Rockefeller Museum, Jerusalem. The lintel originally on the west portal contains figurative scenes of the life of Christ prior to his crucifixion; the one originally on the east portal is dominated by a vine-scroll motif with human and animal figures enmeshed in its spirals. Recent studies have demonstrated that the lintels display stylistic and iconographic associations with architectural sculpture from churches in central Italy.

The Figurative Lintel

Representations of architectural structures divide the western lintel into panels depicting scenes from the life of Christ. The traditional approach reads the lintel as a

The Raising of Lazarus *(detail).*
This event took place in Lazarus's house at
Bethany, represented by a triple-arched and
domed structure. On the right stands Jesus with
an open book in one hand, blessing with the
other. Beside him Martha is raising her hands in
gratitude. On the left two men are rolling the
stone off Lazarus's tomb. Lazarus, who has risen,
stands by the grave, enwrapped with shrouds.

Around him are his neighbors who witnessed the
miracle; some are raising their arms with
amazement, others are holding their hands to
their noses, either to wipe their tears or because
of the bad odor of the dead (John 11:38–44).

Jesus and His Disciples Meet Mary Magdalene and Martha *(detail).*

This event took place at Bethany near Jerusalem. In the center of the scene Jesus, with a crossed halo about his head, stands on a round stone; the stone may have symbolized the Universe, or marked the spot for pilgrims. One of Jesus's arms supports a book; the other is raised, blessing the two veiled women: Martha who is kissing his feet, and Mary who is raising her hands, beseeching the resurrection of the dead Lazarus. On the left, behind the women, are bearded men standing at the city gate. On the right are four of the disciples (John 11:17-33). A different interpretation reads this scene as an apparition of Christ after his resurrection. Kneeling beside him are the Virgin Mary and Mary Magdalene; on the left are pilgrims and on the right are four disciples.

The vine-scroll lintel is dominated by spiraling branches that form round "medallions". Within them are **Naked youths** (extreme "medallions" on the left and right), **Predatory birds** (second "medallions" from the left and right) and **Hybrid figures** (the central "medallion").

Detail of the first "medallion" on the left: three naked male youths are intertwined within the spiraling flora. The youths are holding on to the branches, as if turning the medallion.

*Detail of the central "medallion":
The upper right figure entangled
within the branches is a centaur—
half horse, half man—with his bow
and arrow; on the left is a naked
male youth; below is a harpy with
a human female head and the body
of a bird.*

narrative sequence from left to right. First on the left is the Raising of Lazarus, followed by the Meeting of Jesus and his Disciples with Mary Magdalene and Martha. The two scenes are linked and divided by a city gate. The next panel is divided into two: the lower part displays the Preparation of the Paschal Lamb, the upper part shows the Preparations for the Coming Events. The fourth scene from the left depicts the Bringing of the Ass and the Colt. It is unified with the next scene — the Entry into Jerusalem — by the representation of the Mount of Olives in the background. The Last Supper concludes the sequence.

The order of the scenes and their iconography probably reflect not the chronology of events, but the topography and sequence of the sites a pilgrim would have visited in the mid-twelfth century in and around Jerusalem. All these events were the immediate predecessors of the passion, death, and resurrection of Christ, which are celebrated, and their sites identified, inside the Church of the Holy Sepulchre. The scenes can also be considered as celebratory events, the final and most important of them — Christ's triumph over death — taking place inside the church. Another interpretation, which reads the scenes from the center outward, suggests that the lintel manifests the two natures of Jesus: the human nature, represented by the Entry to Jerusalem and by the Last Supper, and the divine nature, demonstrated by Jesus' apparitions on Earth after his resurrection and by the Raising of Lazarus (see the detailed photographs).

The Vine-scroll Lintel

The eastern lintel is dominated by a thick spiraling branch that forms round "medallions" — five large ones and four pairs of small ones between them. The medallions are adorned with concentric branches crowded with leaves, fruit, and flowers. Within the large medallions are entangled different figures: hybrid figures and a naked youth in the center, predatory birds in the flanking medallions, and naked youths at the two ends (see the detailed photographs). A wavy band frames the lintel.

The themes displayed in the lintel derive from Early Christian art motifs characteristic of the Mediterranean region, which developed and appeared with variations in the twelfth century. It has been argued that the lintel bears a symbolic representation of the fate of sinful men — the naked youths trapped in the coils of hell and threatened by vice and evil, represented by the hybrid figures. Other scholars have suggested that the program of the lintel is based on the motif of the *Arbor Vitae* — the Tree of Life, a symbolic representation of all of creation, redeemed by the sacrifice of Christ.

The Chapel of the Franks

The square domed chapel was built on the east side of the south transept facade. The chapel had two windows with round arches, supported by two columns and framed by a frieze. The windows were set between two cornices located at the same levels as the architectural elements of the church facade: the upper cornice — at the level of the meander cornice and the lower one — at the level of the rosette frieze (see "The South Transept Facade"). A broad concave frieze, composed of intertwining vine scrolls and birds eating grapes, rests above the west window. The frieze over the south window depicts a variation of the same theme with smaller birds perched above a fruit basket among the leaves.

The Chapel of the Franks: note the upper and lower cornices, and the friezes above the windows. Below: the inner tympanum of the Chapel of the Franks, and the mosaic above it.

The north wall of the chapel, which originally served as the entrance to the Calvary Chapel, is now blocked, but the portal itself has been preserved. It was flanked on either side by three columns, surmounted by elaborate acanthus-leaf capitals and a frieze, similar to those of the church facade. The inner tympanum was magnificently decorated with marble relief: scrolls of acanthus, dotted with grape clusters in the lower section, and larger grape clusters hanging from vine scrolls in the upper part. These motifs — grape-vines and birds — have symbolized the Eucharist and Paradise since the early Christian era. Above the portal-tympanum an elaborate mosaic is still visible; it is all that remains of the lavish mosaics which once covered the interior of the chapel.(see "The Mosaics and Frescoes").

Other Architectural Sculpture

The sculptured elements of the Crusader church were executed, in their different styles and techniques, by two or more teams of sculptors. Most of the capitals were adorned with foliate designs, especially acanthus leaves. Several figurative capitals survived, among them double capitals depicting monsters and masks, and the "winged Solomon" capital in the north transept aisle. Six capitals decorated the entrance to the Prison of Christ, including one with the unusual image of "Daniel in the lions' den." Ninety-six corbels, some now broken, were carved almost in the round on the exterior cornice of the Rotunda dome. The corbels bore a rich variety of architectural, geometric, vegetal, and figurative motifs. The latter included heads of human males, a demon, horses, oxen, and an ass.

The Mosaics and Frescoes

Pilgrims' accounts describe the Crusader Church of the Holy Sepulchre gleaming with mosaics, most now lost. The mosaics constituted the main focus of the decorations, in keeping with Byzantine tradition in the region. Their style and technique strongly reflect Eastern Byzantine influences, and — especially in the decorative designs — a local, Muslim tradition. The Rotunda retained its mid-eleventh-century mosaics depicting the figures of Constantine, Helena, the twelve apostles, the twelve prophets, and St. Michael. The image of the Anastasis, which had originally existed in the Rotunda apse, was transferred by the Crusaders to their main apse farther east. The Edicule was decorated with mosaics depicting the Entombment and the Three Marys at the Tomb, and dotted with inscriptions.

The Calvary Chapel complex was covered with mosaics, some done during the Byzantine restoration of 1042–1048, some by the Crusaders during the late 1140s, and others executed later, sometime before 1639. The mosaics included images of the Crucifixion, the Deposition and the Entombment (11th century); the Ascension, figures of the Old Testament, prophets and kings, foliate decoration, and Latin inscriptions (12th century); and images of the Sacrifice of Isaac, the Ascension of Elijah, the Last Supper, the Anastasis, and figures of Helena and Heraclius. Of this impressive mosaic program only a small fragment survives on the vault of today's Franciscan chapel, depicting the ascending Christ within an oval mandorla. Its iconography and stylistic features date the Ascension mosaic to the mid-twelfth century.

The Grotto of the Holy Cross was decorated with eleventh century frescoes, most now lost. The surviving fragment of the Crucifixion image depicts the torso and lower body of Jesus on the cross, flanked by the haloes and shoulders of the Virgin Mary and St. John. The iconography and stylistic features of the Crucifixion fresco are characteristic of mid-twelfth-century Italy.

The exterior of the church was also adorned with mosaics, very little of which survived. One of the portal-tympana of the south transept facade occupied, according to some pilgrims, the images of Christ and Mary Magdalene, but only scant remnants of bleached tesserae can be seen today on the lower part of the east tympanum.

The Chapel of the Franks was lavishly decorated with twelfth-century mosaics, part of which survived above the arched entrance, now blocked, into the Calvary Chapel. The mosaic consisted of four colorful bands of foliate and geometric designs, drawing from Muslim and Byzantine traditions.

A pair of sculptured lions adorns the south cornice of the Chapel of the Franks.

Mosaic depicting the Ascension set on the vault of the Franciscan Chapel of Calvary. This is the most important figurative Crusader mosaic surviving in the Church of the Holy Sepulchre.

The Christian Communities at the Church of the Holy Sepulchre

The Church of the Holy Sepulchre, unlike most other churches, is served not by one, but by a variety of communities. The presence side-by-side of Greek Orthodox, Roman Catholics, Armenians, Syrians, Copts, and Ethiopians in the church and its surroundings creates a unique cosmopolitan atmosphere, enriched by the diverse rituals, clergy costumes, and styles of art and decoration. Upon entering the church, the present-day visitor is likely to be confused by this mixture of different cultural traditions, in which each Christian community emphasizes its typical characteristics. Today, 1665 years after the construction of the first Church of the Holy Sepulchre, the coexistence of six communities on the one site adds a special flavor of cosmopolitan Christian tradition to the church.

The three "great communities" currently represented in the Church of the Holy Sepulchre are the Greek Orthodox, the Latin (Roman Catholic) and the Armenian, among whom the lion's share of the church and its surroundings is divided. Other parts of the church complex are in the possession of, or occupied by, the Copts, the Syrian-Jacobites, and the Ethiopians. The Protestants are allowed to visit but not to hold services in the main church. The development of this allotment has been tightly linked to the history of Christians in Jerusalem in the last seven hundred years, although the presence of a variety of Christian communities in the city goes back to the early Byzantine times.

The inauguration of the first, Constantinian church in A.D. 335 marks the beginning of Christian sovereignty in Jerusalem and the Holy Land. From that time on the Church of the Holy Sepulchre has become the main goal of Christian pilgrimage, and a subject of veneration for the whole Christian world.

Major differences on matters of doctrine first threatened the unity of the Christian church a century later. A major theological conflict broke out in 431 between Cyril, the patriarch of Alexandria, and Nestorios, the patriarch of Constantinople; Nestorios had publicly stressed the human nature of Christ and refused to acknowledge that Mary was the Mother of God. The Ecumenical Council of Ephesus condemned Nestorios who, after seeking refuge in his old monastery in Antioch, was banished to Upper Egypt, where he later died. He had established the Nestorian church, and when soon after, a branch of this church was founded in Jerusalem, it sowed the first seeds of separation in the Christian community.

A much more serious split occurred in A.D. 451, when the Council of Chalcedon affirmed that Christ had two natures, divine and human. Following this decision the main Christian norm was declared "Orthodox" (in Greek: orthos = correct, doxa = opinion), as opposed to "Monophysites" (in Greek: monos = one, physis = nature) who claimed that the incarnate Christ had a single, indivisible nature. This theological dispute was the immediate cause of a major break, which led to the evolution of the different Monophysite churches — the Armenian, Coptic, Syrian-Jacobite, and Ethiopian churches. The division between the churches has been

A map of the community division of the Church of the Holy Sepulchre following the Status Quo agreement of 1852. This plan, based on the measurements of Conrad Schick at the end of the 19th century, demonstrates the complexity of the physical relationships between the denominations occupying the church.

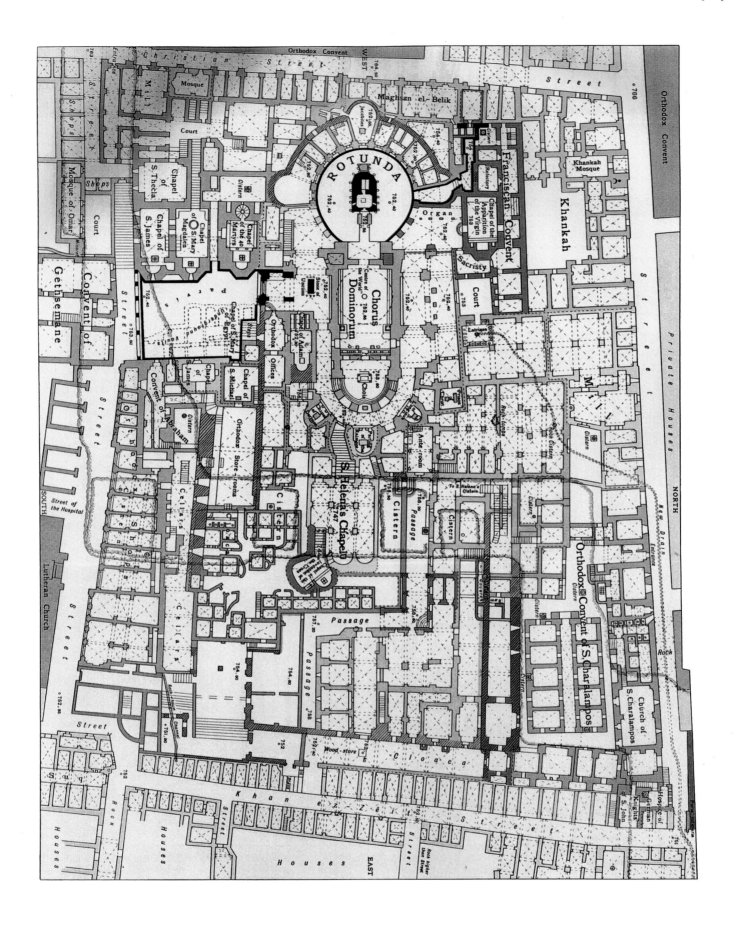

Orthodox Convent

Christian Street

WEST

Street

Orthodox Convent

Maghsan-el-Belik

Mosque

Court

Shops

ROTUNDA

Khankah Mosque

Chapel of S. Thecla

Chapel of S. James

Chapel of S. Mary Magdalen

Chapel of the 40 Martyrs

Franciscan Convent

Refectory

Khankah

Chapel of the Apparition of the Virgin

Organ

Court

Sacristy

Chorus Dominorum

Centre of the World

Stone of Unction

Chapel of S. Mary the Egyptian

Chapel of Adam

Chapel of S. Michael

Orthodox Offices

Orthodox Store-rooms

Convent of Abraham

Chapel of S. James

Cistern

Latrines

To S. Helena's Cistern

Convent of Gethsemane

Street

Street

Mosque of Omar

Court

S. Helena's Chapel

Cistern

Passage

Cistern

Cistern

Cistern

Cistern

Cistern

Orthodox Convent of S. Charalampos

Cellars

Cistern

Street of the Hospital

SOUTH

Cellars

Shops

Lutheran Church

Street

Passage

Wood-store

Passage

Cloaca

Church of S. Charalampos

Church of S. Charalampos

Knights of S. John

Hospice of German Knights of S. John

Street

Houses

Suq

Rock

Houses

Street

Khan ez-Zêt

Street

Houses

EAST

Mill

Street

Private Houses

NORTH

New Drain Entrance

Rock

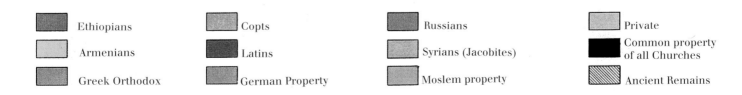

	Ethiopians		Copts		Russians		Private
	Armenians		Latins		Syrians (Jacobites)		Common property of all Churches
	Greek Orthodox		German Property		Moslem property		Ancient Remains

85

strictly observed ever since, and is reflected in the allotment of religious rights and properties in the Church of the Holy Sepulchre.

There is no concrete evidence of the internal division of the Church of the Holy Sepulchre between the Christian congregations during Byzantine and early Islamic times when the church was under the authority of the Jerusalem patriarchate, which represented the main stream of Eastern Christianity. However, certain agreements might have existed with the Nestorian and Monophysite communities in Jerusalem on the right to conduct ceremonies at the church.

The development of the Roman Catholic Church in Italy and Western Europe in the Early Middle Ages, and the rivalry that arose between Rome and Constantinople over the question of religious leadership, caused the major schism between Eastern (later Greek Orthodox) and Western (later Roman Catholic or Latin) branches of Christianity. This schism, which had already formulated in the ninth and tenth centuries, resulted in a final split in 1054, when Michael Cerularius, the patriarch of Constantinople, officially refused to accept the supreme authority of the pope in Rome. From that time on the Greek Orthodox church and the Roman Catholic church no longer considered each other variations of the one true church. This formal schism also paved the way for the establishment of the Latin patriarchate in Jerusalem immediately after the Crusader invasion of the city in 1099, and to a dispute between the Latin and the Greek Orthodox communities on their property rights at the Church of the Holy Sepulchre.

Seated on the Patriarchal throne, His Eminence Vassilius Senior Metropolitan of Caesarea officiates Mass for the Greek Orthodox community.

Although the Latin presence in Jerusalem was already established in the ninth century, the Latins did not share the ownership of the Church of the Holy Sepulchre prior to the Crusader domination. Soon after the foundation of Crusader rule over Jerusalem, a Latin patriarch was appointed and the Greek Orthodox patriarch left the city for residence abroad. The Church of the Holy Sepulchre was transformed into a Latin church, the western impact expressed in the rebuilding of the church by the Crusaders. But Latin authority in the church did not last for long. The conquest of Jerusalem by Saladin in 1187 put an end to the Christian sovereignty in the church, and opened the way for its internal division between the different Christian communities. Following Saladin's conquest the Muslim authorities demanded heavy taxes for the rights of possession given to the various Christian communities at the Church of the Holy Sepulchre. They also handed over the keys of the church — for the first time in its history — to a Muslim family. At the same time, Saladin reestablished the privileges of the Greek Orthodox patriarchate, and his administration gave preference to the recently founded Coptic presence at the church.

The roots of the present-day division of the church between the different denominations go back to the thirteenth century. The establishment of the Armenian patriarchate, the Coptic bishopric, and the Ethiopian church, together with the increasing influence of the Georgians in the Christian community of Jerusalem, all led to the first formal allotment of properties within the church. The penetration of the Franciscan friars to Jerusalem as representatives of the Latin community added another component to this struggle for influence in the church and surroundings.

Between the fourteenth and sixteenth centuries, properties and rights in the church complex shifted several times: the Franciscans were given rights in the Edicule and the Chapel of Apparition, as well as at the monastery northwest of the church; the Greeks possessed the Katholikon and the Prison of Christ; the Syrians had rights on the Chapel of Helena and the Stone of Unction; the Armenians established their possession in the south part of the Rotunda of the Anastasis; the Copts constructed a small chapel adjacent to the Edicule; the Georgians were granted large parts of Calvary, and for some time possessed the keys to the church; the Ethiopians were also present inside the church and had the rights of use in certain areas.

The conquest of Jerusalem by the Ottomans in 1516 affected the struggles for possession

*Pilgrims from the Greek Islands
rest on the Parvis stairs during
Easter.*

in the Church of the Holy Sepulchre. During the seventeenth century the Greek Orthodox, the Latins, and the Armenians extended their properties in the church at the expense of the other communities, who could not afford to pay the high taxes required by the Ottoman authorities, and were forced to leave the church and sell their rights. Thus the Greek Orthodox got parts of Calvary and the Stone of Unction, and the Latins were granted rights on Calvary, in the north transept (the "seven arches of the Virgin"), and in the Chapel of the Holy Cross.

The renovations of the church were also the cause for disputes between the communities; the Franciscans were granted Ottoman permission to restore the Edicule in 1555 and the dome of the church in 1719, and the Greek Orthodox took charge of the major restoration project that followed the destructive fire of 1808.

Minor disputes leading to changes of ownership between the congregations lasted until the mid-nineteenth century, when the official allotment of sections in the Church of the Holy Sepulchre between the different communities was established. A special declaration, presenting what had become known as the Status Quo, was issued in 1852 by the Ottoman regime. This allotment, which has been maintained ever since, ensured Greek Orthodox control over the largest part of the church (see the plan on page 85). The most important areas of the church were declared common property: the Edicule, the floor of the Rotunda and its dome, and the Parvis and entrance to the church.

The Greek Orthodox patriarchate has possession of the main church (the Katholikon), two of the three chapels in the ambulatory, the north part of Calvary, the Prison of Christ at the northeast corner of the church, and most of the rooms surrounding the Rotunda of the Anastasis. They also possess some of the buildings around the Parvis, the monastery of St. Abraham, and the belfry.

The Latins hold possession of most of the northwest section of the complex, in the center of which the Chapel of Apparition is located. They are also responsible for the south part of Calvary, the Chapel of Mary's Agony, and the Chapel of the Invention of the Cross.

The Armenians are in charge of the Chapel of St. Helena, the Station of the Holy Women, the south galleries and one of the rooms around the Rotunda, the Chapel of the Parting of the Raiment in the ambulatory, and the Chapel of St. John at the east part of the Parvis.

The Syrians have the right to use the Chapel of Nicodemus and the adjacent rock-cut tomb of Joseph of Arimathea.

The Copts possess the small chapel attached to the west end of the Edicule; two rooms in the Rotunda (south of the Chapel of Nicodemus), and a two-storied structure — residence for Coptic deacons, west of the main church gate. Northeast of the church is the Coptic Patriarchate, and a few buildings nearby are also under Coptic possession.

The Ethiopians have no rights within the church, but they dominate the courtyard of Deir es-Sultan ("the African Village") and the two chapels to the east of the Parvis: the Chapel of St. Michael and the Chapel of the Four Beasts.

The Greek Orthodox

The Greek Orthodox community is today the largest of the Christian denominations in Jerusalem, and considered to be the descendant of the earliest Christians in the city. The bishopric of Jerusalem, founded late in the first century A.D., was recognized as the first church of ancient Christianity. However, the church and the community lost their leading role during the second and third centuries. Only with the rediscovery of the Holy Places in Jerusalem and the construction of the Church of the Holy Sepulchre in the fourth century did the Jerusalem church restore its central role in the religious life of Christian Palestine.

The major position of the Jerusalem church was finally recognized by the Ecumenical Council of Chalcedon in A.D. 451, when the bishop of Jerusalem was appointed patriarch. The

Jerusalem patriarchate was then proclaimed the fifth patriarchate of the Byzantine Empire, joining Rome, Alexandria, Antioch, and Constantinople.

In the fifth and sixth centuries the patriarchate of Jerusalem flourished. About sixty bishoprics were under its domain, including hundreds of churches and monasteries spread all over the country. Following the Islamic conquest of Palestine in 638 the patriarch of Jerusalem, although much weakened, was still considered by the Muslim authorities to be the leading representative of the Christian communities. Thus the patriarch held broad authority over the social and economic concerns of the Christian population of Palestine.

The sovereignty of the Orthodox patriarchate over the Christian communities came to an end with the Crusader conquest of Palestine in 1099 and the establishment of the Latin patriarchate. In the twelfth century the Greek Orthodox patriarchs resided outside Jerusalem, and returned to the city only after the end of the Crusader period.

The Crusaders' retreat from Palestine saw the decline of Christian institutions and rehabilitation was slow. The establishment of the Armenian patriarchate and the Coptic, Syrian, and Ethiopian independent churches weakened even further the leading position of the Greek Orthodox patriarchate. Although the Byzantine emperors intervened time and again on behalf of the Greek Orthodox, only under the Ottoman regime did the Greek Orthodox patriarchate restore some of its power.

A view of the Rotunda and a part of the Chapel of the Apparition.

Following the destructive fire in 1808 at the Church of the Holy Sepulchre, the Ottoman regime granted the Greek Orthodox patriarchate the permission to restore the church at the expense of the Greek and Russian nations. The present-day Greek Orthodox patriarchate numbers about 150 monks ranking from the patriarch to young novices. The presiding patriarch — Deodoros I — is the ninety-sixth in succession. At his side is a Holy Synod of fourteen members, ranking from metropolitan to archimandrite.

The Greek Orthodox patriarchate has under its possession large parts of the Holy Sepulchre compound, and it is also the owner of twenty-three additional monasteries in the Old City of Jerusalem and its surroundings. The present-day patriarchate complex, established in the nineteenth century, is located west of the Church of the Holy Sepulchre, and covers about seven-and-one-half acres. Within it are the administrative center, the patriarch's office and reception hall, and a hostel for pilgrims.

The Roman Catholics

The Roman Catholic or Latin presence in Jerusalem was established following the Crusader invasion in 1099, although Latin interests in the city were expressed even earlier. The main trigger for Latin penetration of Jerusalem was the involvement of Charlemagne in the construction of churches and monasteries in the city in the early ninth century. The establishment of Latin churches in the Muristan area, south of the Holy Sepulchre, during the eleventh century provided the first significant Latin foothold in this area. The first Latin patriarchate of Jerusalem was founded on the first of August 1099, only two weeks after the Crusader conquest of the city. However, it survived only eighty-eight years: following the defeat of the Crusaders at the battle of the Horns of Hattin and the Islamic conquest of Jerusalem by Saladin in 1187, the Latins were forced to leave the city and most of their churches and monasteries were converted to mosques. Only a handful of Latin priests were granted permission to officiate in the Church of the Holy Sepulchre.

A devotional picture of the agony of the Virgin above the altar in the Latin Chapel of the Franks.

The Roman Catholic presence in Jerusalem renewed its power in the fourteenth century, spearheaded by the Franciscan friars, who had been entrusted with the guardianship of the holy places, thus creating the "Custody of the Holy Land" with a custos or custodian presiding.

Founded in 1209 by Saint Francis of Assisi, the Franciscan order (the Order of Friars Minors) spread rapidly all over Europe and overseas. The Franciscans arrived in Palestine in

1335, after receiving the Sultan's official permission (*firman*) to settle in Jerusalem, to live permanently in the Church of the Holy Sepulchre, and to celebrate Mass and other acts of public worship there. In 1342 the Custody was officially charged by the Holy See with the guardianship, maintenance, and protection of the Holy Places.

A long and steady effort to gain more control of the Holy Places, in which the Franciscan friars were very active on behalf of the Latin community, evolved following the establishment of Franciscan presence in Jerusalem. During the Ottoman period many sites in Jerusalem and its surroundings came into Latin possession, among them considerable parts of the Church of the Holy Sepulchre.

These trends were intensified during the second half of the nineteenth century, with the increasingly significant role of Jerusalem and the Holy Places in international politics and the growing numbers of tourists and pilgrims. The reestablishment of the Latin patriarchate in 1847 played a major role in expanding the Roman Catholic influence in Jerusalem.

The Latin patriarchate of Jerusalem has today under its authority numerous religious institutions, the most famous of them being the Franciscan Custody of the Holy Land. Others include the Carmelites who are in charge of the sanctuaries of Mount Carmel, the Dominicans who established the École Biblique of St. Stephen in Jerusalem, the Benedictines who possess the Dormition Abbey on Mount Zion, and the Trappists of the Monastery of Latrun.

The Armenians

The Armenian congregation of Jerusalem is one of the oldest in the city and its roots go back to the first days of the establishment of Christianity as the leading religion of Palestine in the fourth century A.D. The Armenian church, which has clear national characteristics, has succeeded in keeping its special character throughout the centuries.

Archaeological evidence pointing to the early Armenian presence in Jerusalem has been found in various places in and around the city. Several ancient monasteries from the fifth to the eighth centuries were discovered north of the Damascus Gate and on the slopes of the Mount of Olives. A list of monasteries and churches in the Holy Land, composed in the seventh century, describes some seventy Armenian monasteries and churches around Jerusalem.

The Armenian presence in Jerusalem continued and developed uninterruptedly through the ages. The construction of St. James Cathedral, probably in the eleventh century, established the Armenian quarter of Jerusalem in its present location in the southwest part of the Old City. The Armenians were the only Christian community that remained in its place and in possession of their property following Saladin's conquest. With the official establishment of the Armenian patriarchate in 1311, the patriarch was made the protector of the Monophysite communities in Jerusalem, a position that was confirmed in the sixteenth century by the Ottoman Sultan Selim I.

The Armenians in Jerusalem have throughout the years preserved their ties with the cultural heritage of their geographical homeland in Armenia, and are thus tightly united in common language, costume, and ethno-religious identity. Throughout the centuries the Armenians of Jerusalem were involved in the safekeeping of their rights in the Holy Places and especially in the Church of the Holy Sepulchre, and they assisted the numerous Armenian pilgrims who visited the city, many of them with the purpose of staying in Jerusalem for good.

The Armenian patriarchate was organized as a monastic brotherhood, named St. James Brotherhood, after St. James the Major, the patron saint of the Armenian church in Jerusalem. It is headed by the patriarch and composed of five bishops, thirty-two archimandrites, and about seventy lay monks, most of them living within the boundaries of the Armenian quarter.

The Armenian quarter in the Old City is a closed compound accessed through a single gate, which is closed at night. It was built around St. James Cathedral, which is also the seat of the patriarch. Religious and cultural institutes are located within the compound, as well as

Armenian choirboys and deacons, candles in hand, stand before an Armenian prelate during one of the Easter processions in front of the Tomb of Christ.

schools and living quarters. Originally inhabited by monks and priests involved in the safekeeping of the Holy Places, the present-day Armenian quarter, with its tradition-conscious community, still keeps its unique atmosphere.

During the nineteenth and twentieth centuries the Armenian population of Jerusalem has increased due to the emigration of secular Armenians from their homeland to Jerusalem, supporting the existing Armenian community both demographically and economically. The present-day Armenian community of Jerusalem presents a coexistence between the religious clergy and the secular congregation that lives within and around the Armenian quarter. This combination of religious and national community provides the Armenians in Jerusalem with their unique position among the Christian congregations.

The Syrians

The Syrian-Jacobite church is one of the oldest, although smallest, among the congregations in Jerusalem. The liturgical language of the Syrian community is still the ancient Syriac, closely akin to the Aramaic spoken by the Jews in the time of Jesus. The use of the Syriac language in the Byzantine Church of the Holy Sepulchre is attested by Egeria, a pilgrim visiting Jerusalem around A.D. 385 (see above, pg. 38-39), who noted that the native Syrian, along with Greek, was used at the ceremonies in the church.

The Syrian community in Jerusalem flourished during Byzantine and early medieval times. The Syrian church was among the adherents of Monophsitism following the Council of Chalcedon in 451. The position of the church was strengthened with the activities of Jacob Baradeus in the sixth century, and it was in recognition of his work that the Syrian church is also called the Jacobite.

Syrian bishops are said to have been residing in Jerusalem since the middle of the twelfth century. The present seat of the Syrian Orthodox bishop of Jerusalem, at the church and monastery of St. Mark in the Old City, was built, according to the Syrian tradition, over the ruins of the site of the Last Supper.

The Copts

Coptic presence in Jerusalem dates back to early Byzantine times, when pilgrims and monks from Egypt traveled to Jerusalem and settled in the city. The Egyptian monk St. Hillarion, a disciple of St. Anthony, was one of the Christians to proselytize among the heathen of Roman Palestine. The pilgrims Paula and Egeria (late fourth century) mention the presence of Egyptian monks in the Church of the Holy Sepulchre.

After the Ecumenical Council of Chalcedon in 451, the Coptic church became an autonomous Monophysite church. The Coptic presence in Jerusalem made itself increasingly felt during the early Middle Ages, with the construction of a number of Coptic churches in the city. But this development stopped during the Crusader period, when the Copts were not allowed to visit or reside in Jerusalem.

After the conquest of Jerusalem by Saladin in 1187, the Church of the Holy Sepulchre was reopened for Coptic pilgrimage, and most of the Coptic properties in the city were restored. The improved standing of the Copts under Saladin and his successors was achieved because many Copts served in administrative capacities in his staff. In 1236 the Coptic Orthodox patriarchate of the See of Jerusalem and the Near East was established, and Patriarch Cyril III of Alexandria appointed Anba Basilios I as archbishop in Jerusalem.

The strong position held by the Copts in Jerusalem during the Middle Ages can be seen in the rights the community gained at the Church of the Holy Sepulchre: from the fourteenth century on Coptic monks were granted permission to live within the church. In 1537 the Copts constructed a small chapel behind the Edicule. Today, this chapel constitutes the most

His Eminence Mar Swerios Malki Murad, Syrian Orthodox Metropolitan and Patriarchal Vicar of Jerusalem, Jordan and Holy Land leads his community in prayer.

Entrance to the Coptic Patriarchate at the 9th station of the Cross marking the place where Jesus stumbled for the third time.

important shrine possessed by the Copts. The Coptic connections with the Monastery of Deir es-Sultan and its adjacent chapels go back to the thirteenth century, although it is difficult to establish the respective shares of Copts and Ethiopians in this area. The two chapels located between the Parvis and Deir es-Sultan were possessed by the Copts and today are used by the Ethiopians. Both are located within Crusader structures: the Chapel of Michael the Archangel (the one near the Parvis) is one of the oldest chapels adjacent to the church. The upper chapel — the Chapel of the Four Beasts of the Revelation — is named after the six-winged creatures set beside heaven's throne referred to in the last book of the New Testament (4:6–10).

The Coptic patriarchate building, located to the northeast of the Church of the Holy Sepulchre, is the official headquarters and residence of the patriarch. The building was constructed in the second half of the nineteenth century, together with the Church of St. Anthony, which serves as the main Coptic community church in Jerusalem.

The Ethiopians

Tha small present–day Ethiopian presence in the Church of the Holy Sepulchre is concentrated on the roof of the Chapel of St Helena.

The documentation of Ethiopian Christians goes back to the earliest days of Christianity. An Ethiopian is mentioned in the Acts of the Apostles (8:6–9) among those who accepted the teaching of Christ and were baptized on the way to Jerusalem. During the Byzantine and medieval periods the presence of Ethiopian monks and the visits of Ethiopian pilgrims to the Holy Land and Jerusalem were frequently mentioned. In the fifteenth century the Ethiopians possessed one of the chapels in the ambulatory of the Church of the Holy Sepulchre and for a time they also owned the Chapel of St. Helena. But in the seventeenth century the Ethiopians could not afford to pay the exactions of the Ottoman regime, and they lost all their holdings within the church.

The small present-day Ethiopian presence in the Church of the Holy Sepulchre is concentrated on the roof of the Chapel of St. Helena, where some twenty-five monks live in small, humble huts, with tiny windows and low doors. This African-style village, which is actually a monastery for Ethiopian monks, is called Deir es-Sultan (the monastery of the emperor) commemorating the Ethiopian tradition that associates the site with the biblical king Solomon, who had presented it as a gift to the Ethiopian queen of Sheba. It is not known when the site was inhabited by Ethiopians, but descriptions from the sixteenth and seventeenth centuries tell about the Ethiopian monks living at the village. The small Ethiopian community during this period was actually under the protection of the Greek Orthodox patriarchate of Jerusalem.

The passage from Deir es-Sultan to the main entrance of the Church of the Holy Sepulchre is through two chapels that are today used by the Ethiopians: the Chapel of the Four Beasts in the upper level and the Chapel of St. Michael in a lower level. Both chapels are part of a Crusader structure that connected the Parvis and the Canons' cloister. The chapels are decorated with Ethiopian-style icons and cloths, and in an adjacent small room the clergy uniforms are stored.

The Ethiopian community of Jerusalem was almost eliminated following a plague that hit the city in 1838. Most of the monks perished and the village was deserted for several years. When the Ethiopians came back to settle at the site, it was held by the Coptic patriarchate, and the newcomers lived there as "guests" of the Copts, a situation that has since then been as a source of dispute between the two communities.

In the late nineteenth century the Ethiopian community of Jerusalem succeeded in enlarging its properties and population. The "African Village" was settled once again and other properties were bought in the Old City and in West Jerusalem. The Ethiopian monastery of Deir es-Sultan remains the most sacred site for the Ethiopian community, and to live amid the humble dwellings of the African Village is a high religious privilege.

The Liturgy at the Church of the Holy Sepulchre

The Holy Sepulchre revolves around the story of the crucifixion, burial, and resurrection of Christ. This narrative and the associated theological determinations were used by the builders of the church to create a physical environment that follows in a material fashion the last day of Christ on this earth. The Church of the Holy Sepulchre is thus the tangible culmination of the passage of Christ, from his trial by Pontius Pilate either at the Citadel or at the Antonia Fortress, which was located alongside the Temple, along the nine stations of the cross on the Via Dolorosa to the five final stations, all included within the precincts of the church. If the church is the corporeal representation of this last day, the liturgy, and especially that of the Holy Week of Easter, is their ceremonial representation. Indeed, the church comes to life during Easter, as its central theme becomes all the more appropriate. During this time the communities play out, day by day, the last week of Christ in graphic displays of devotion that clearly explain the Easter passion to the faithful. It is worth noting that Christmas has little relevance for the Holy Sepulchre, its halls emptying as the clergy migrate south to the services held in the Church of the Nativity in Bethlehem.

As the Catholic (Latin) and Orthodox churches use the Gregorian and Julian calendars respectively, the Holy Weeks are not always concurrent. Easter for the Latins is set for the first full moon after the spring equinox and thus changes from year to year. The different calculations of the Julian calendar used by the Orthodox churches sometimes result in Easter falling on the same day as that of the Latins, though it is usually a week or two after them. Thus the Passion of Christ is reenacted as many times as there are communities. The Easter liturgy clearly displays the theological, but especially the cultural differences of the three major and three minor communities active in the Church of the Holy Sepulchre. As the events of Easter are intensive, involving hundreds of clergy and thousands of believers in a complex of processions, masses, and services, the division of both time and space is highly organized in accordance with the decisions of the Status Quo committee of the Church of the Holy Sepulchre. A detailed timetable of events has been drawn up and signed as a contract between the three great communities: the Greek Orthodox, the Latins, and the Armenians. The strict observation of the schedules and directions set out in the timetable is necessary in order to prevent any unfortunate conflagrations between the communities. To officiate over the full observance of the program, the sacristans of the different communities are always present during the services of the others, and stand on either side of the entrance to the Edicule throughout the liturgy of the other churches.

The Procession

A basic feature of all services is the procession. These start from the respective patriarchates: the Armenians proceeding from the Cathedral of St. James in the Armenian quarter, via the

A Latin procession through the streets of the old city of Jerusalem is led by the kavass *who rhythmically strike the pavement with their staffs.*

Citadel, David Street, and Christian Quarter Street to the Church of the Holy Sepulchre; the Latin patriarch — from his residence near Jaffa Gate, through the markets of David and Christian Quarter Street; the Franciscan custos proceeds from St. Saviour Convent near the New Gate, down through St. Francis Street and Christian Quarter Street; the Greek patriarch — from his patriarchate in the heart of the Christian quarter, through Christian Quarter Street; the Coptic archbishop proceeds from his residence to the north of the Holy Sepulchre compound, via Deir es-Sultan and the Ethiopian Chapel of St. Michael; and finally the Syrian Orthodox — from St. Mark's Cathedral along the road by that name and through Christian Quarter Street. The processions are led by two to four *kavass*, as designated by the Status Quo committee. This title is a remnant of the Ottoman period, the *kavass* being a steward, either dressed in an elaborately embroidered costume dating to Turkish rule, or in a khaki police-like uniform from the British Mandate period. On his head is a burgundy felt fez, and a heavy, silver-tipped staff is held in one hand. The staff is rhythmically pounded on the pavement thus warning passers-by of the arrival of the procession, to ensure that the path is cleared for the patriarch and his entourage. Following the *kavass* are the clergy, usually arranged by hierarchy: led by the choirboys are the novices, deacons, priests, monks, archimandrites, bishops, archbishops, metropolitans, senior metropolitans, and finally the patriarch himself, usually with a shepherd's crook in his hand (Latin), or a staff crowned with a silver cross flanked by two vipers (Orthodox). Heading the procession at this stage will generally be a large crucifix, the participants following and entering the church dressed in their regular robes.

Upon entering, the patriarchs kneel before the Unction Stone. On this stone the body of Christ, having been taken down from the cross, is said to have been cleaned, anointed, and wrapped in a shroud in accordance with Jewish tradition. The Unction Stone is topped by a row of oil lamps and three candelabra, one from each major community, to either side. The stone is sprinkled with rose water and petals and the patriarchs kiss it before proceeding to their respective chapels. The Latins move to the Chapel of the Apparition, the Greeks to the Katholikon, the Armenians to the southern gallery, the Copts to the chapel behind the Edicule, and the Syrians to the Chapel of Nicodemus. The Ethiopians, having no rights within the church, conduct all the sacraments in their chapels or on the roof above the Chapel of St. Helena.

After entering their denominational chapels, the clergy change into ceremonial vestments; a different wardrobe is used for each day of Easter. These magnificent gowns in bright colors clearly distinguish the clergy from the dowdily dressed laity. The high clergy especially have exquisitely embroidered robes. The Orthodox leaders wear gold crowns decorated with jewels and enameled panels, while the Latin patriarch is fitted with a golden mitre. Once enrobed, the procession announced by the *kavass*, leaves the restricted community areas, and in devotional song moves around the floor of the church to the holy sites commemorated in the Church of the Holy Sepulchre. Behind the *kavass* usually pace deacons or novices carrying banners which display biblical imagery, including scenes from the Gospels and also scenes from the home country of the church. The junior clergy bear a large crucifix, an elaborately bound Bible, and the sacramental vessels appropriate for the specific service. Following them, again in hierarchical order, are the rest of the clergy and finally the patriarch. The route taken by the processions usually includes a visit to Calvary, the Unction Stone, and finally a number of circuits around the Edicule in the Rotunda. Some processions also make their way around the Katholikon ambulatory to attend the small chapels located there. After most processions a mass or service is held in front of the Edicule. From there the procession moves to the community areas where the ceremonial gowns are removed and the procession returns to the residences of the patriarchs.

The song and language of prayer, as well as the clothing sharply distinguish the cultural differences between the communities. Whether it is plain song of hymns in Latin accompanied by the organ; Byzantine open song in Greek or Armenian; hymns in classical Arabic by the Copts; Aramaic or Syriac, the language spoken at the time of Jesus, by the Syrians; or Geez, an ancient predecessor of Amharic, by the Ethiopians, all recite prayers, psalms, and extracts from the appropriate sections of the New Testament. Even with so much in common, the diversity of these cultures brings a special quality to the Church of the Holy Sepulchre, making a visit to the church at Easter an unforgettable experience.

Holy Week

Easter, or Holy Week, as we have described above, is the most important liturgical feast at the church. Thousands of pilgrims arrive for the ceremonies and especially for the two weekends, marked by Palm Sunday and Easter Sunday. Easter has special significance for the Orthodox churches and large numbers of pilgrims travel to Jerusalem from Greece, Cyprus, and Russia. The city becomes, for a few days at least, an Orthodox city, as black-clad grandmothers from the Mediterranean Islands fill the interior of the church in anticipation especially of the miraculous events of the Holy Fire on Holy Saturday.

The Palm Processions and Palm Sunday

The events of Holy Week commence with the ceremonies associated with Palm Sunday, but observance of the passage of Christ from Bethany and Bethphage on his way to Jerusalem is initiated on the Saturday before Palm Sunday, called "Lazarus Saturday" by the Orthodox, when the visit of Christ in Bethany is celebrated. Here Jesus raised Lazarus from the dead, telling Martha, the sister of Lazarus:

> I am the resurrection, and the life: he that believeth in me, though he were dead, yet shall he live (John 11:25).

> Then Jesus six days before the passover came to Bethany, where Lazarus was which had been dead, whom he had raised from the dead (John 12:1).

Jesus probably stayed in Bethany for a week and then proceeded, as related by Luke, to Jerusalem via the nearby village of Bethphage.

On Palm Sunday a priest joins monks and nuns of the Roman Catholic Church in the procession from the Mount of Olives.

And it came to pass, when was come nigh to Bethphage and Bethany, at the mount called the Mount of Olives, he sent two of his disciples, Saying, Go ye into the village over against you; in the which at your entering ye shall find a colt tied, wheron yet never man sat; loose him, and bring him hither. And if any man ask you, Why do ye loose him? thus ye shall say unto him, Because the Lord hath need of him. And they that were sent went their way, and found even as he had said unto them. And as they were loosing the colt, the owners therof said unto them, Why loose ye the colt? And they said, the Lord hath need of him. And they brought him to Jesus: and they cast their garments upon the colt, and they set Jesus theron. And as he went, they spread their clothes in the way. And when he was come nigh, even now at the descent of the mount of Olives, the whole multitude of the disciples began to rejoice and praise God with a loud voice for all the mighty works that they had seen; Saying, Blessed be the King that cometh in the name of the Lord: peace in heaven, and glory in the highest (Luke 19:29–38).

Thus the Easter liturgy for the Greek Orthodox begins with a service in Bethany, the home of Lazarus. In contrast the Latin pilgrimage sets out from the patriarchate to the Franciscan church at Bethphage. Following the pilgrimage the Latin patriarch conducts a procession within the Church of the Holy Sepulchre, starting with the ceremony of the "Solemn Entry" and the opening of the church, which conforms to a strict ritual set by the Status Quo agreement. This ceremony is fully described in the timetable of the services:

12:20 p.m. The Latin sacristan, representing the three communities, leaves his residence in one of the rooms attached to the basilica of the Holy Sepulchre, and calls the Muslim gatekeeper. The gatekeeper arrives.

12:25 p.m. The Latin sacristan rings the bells of the door of the Holy Sepulchre in the following order: a) the Latin bell, b) the Greek bell, c) the Armenian bell, d) the Coptic bell.

12:30 p.m. Solemn Entry. The Latin sacristan passes the ladder to the gatekeeper through a hatch in the door. [The gatekeeper then climbs the ladder and unlocks the two ancient padlocks that seal the double doors of the church.] He then opens the bolt. The Latin sacristan opens the first leaf of the door, the gatekeeper places the ladder behind the door, beside the cord of the Greek bell. The gatekeeper then swings open the second leaf of the door.

This detailed list of actions is carefully followed when opening the door of the church, whether by the Latins, the Greeks, or the Armenians.

His Eminence Archbishop Doctor Anba Abraham, Coptic Orthodox Metropolitan of Jerusalem and the Near East in the Parvis on Palm Sunday.

Some two hours later His Beatitude the Latin patriarch proceeds though the streets of Jerusalem toward the church. A cushion has been placed before the Unction Stone and the Latin candles beside the stone are lit. On entry the patriarch places a mitre on his head and kneels before the stone to kiss it. The stone is then incensed and sprinkled with holy water. On its way to the Chapel of the Apparition the procession forms in the following order: the *kavass*, the bearers of incense and of the crucifix, the standard bearer of St. Francis, four candelabra carriers, the Franciscan monks and finally the beautifully robed patriarch. Leaving the Chapel of the Apparition, the two hours long procession then goes in turn to the Altar of the Holy Sacrament, the Altar of the Column, the Prison of Christ, the Altar of the Parting of the Raiment, the Grotto of the Invention of the Cross, the Chapel of St. Helena, the Altar of the Derision of Christ, the place of the Crucifixion, the Altar of the Nailing to the Cross, the Altar of Our Lady of Sorrows, the Unction Stone, three turns around the Edicule, the Tomb of Christ, the Altar of Mary Magdalene, and finally back to the Chapel of the Apparition. Similar processions are conducted throughout Holy Week by all the communities in a number of variants.

After conducting a service in the Katholikon in the afternoon, His Beatitude the Greek Orthodox patriarch heads the Palm Sunday procession from Bethphage on the Mount of Olives, through the village of et-Tur, down the west slope of the Mount of Olives, and past the Church of Dominus Flevit, its name commemorating the place where the "Lord wept" over his prophecy of the destruction of Jerusalem (Luke 19:41). The patriarch, accompanied by the Orthodox community carrying palm fronds, passes over the Kidron Valley to the Monastery of St. Anne inside St. Stephen's Gate. This path from Bethphage to Jerusalem marks that made by Christ, and it is followed on Palm Sunday by the Latins. The lay community leads the Catholic procession, culminating with His Beatitude the Latin patriarch, His Eminence the Vicar General of the Latin patriarch of Jerusalem, and the Most Reverend Custos of the Holy Land who leads the Franciscans. Following, as a remnant of Crusader times, is the Equestrian Order of the Church of the Holy Sepulchre, instituted by Godfrey of Bouillon in 1099. They are robed in white capes decorated with a large red Franciscan cross and wear oversize berets of velvet felt.

This Palm Sunday procession follows an early tradition. It was described in the fourth century by the pilgrim Egeria:

> The people [...] go down on foot the whole way from the summit of the Mount of Olives. The People go before the Bishop and sing, "Blessed be he who comes in the name of the Lord" [Matthew 21:9] and the children hold branches of palm trees and of olive trees. Thus [...] they come back to the city [...].

Today seventeen centuries later, the Palm Sunday procession is identical, forming a highlight for the laity who are otherwise passive viewers of the proceedings. The procession is especially important for the schools and scout troops of the local Christian communities, who march in song to St. Anne's and then return to the sound of drum and bagpipe bands through the streets of Jerusalem to the patriarchates in the Christian quarter.

The main liturgy of Palm Sunday is conducted within the Church of the Holy Sepulchre. Here for the first time all services are conducted by the five communities with rights within the church. If the dates according to the calendar are not concurrent, the Latins may for example be celebrating Easter Sunday at the same time that the Eastern churches are observing Palm Sunday. This means that a continual stream of processions, patriarchal entries, services, and masses take place throughout the day, changing the interior of the church in every manner minute by minute.

Palm Sunday starts with the entry of the Armenian patriarchal vicar, the chief clergyman of Jerusalem's Armenian community, to the Calvary gallery at 5:30 a.m. for a service in the Armenian gallery. This marks the beginning of the community entries. Next to arrive at 7:00 a.m. is the Latin patriarch who blesses the palms in a service in front of the Edicule. Then the patriarch conducts a procession three times around the Edicule, and thence to the Chapel of the Apparition, before conducting Mass in front of the Edicule. At 7:30 a.m. the Greek patriarch enters the church, proceeding to the Katholikon through the side entrance, because the Latins are conducting a simultaneous service beside the main entrance opposite the tomb. At the time of the Latin mass, the Coptic and Syrian churches also enter the Rotunda, proceeding to their sections of the building, behind the tomb and in the Chapel of Nicodemus. At 8:00 a.m. the Armenian patriarch enters the edifice and makes his way directly to the Armenian gallery, south of the Edicule. At this stage five services are being conducted concurrently only a few meters from one another. This creates a festive cacophony of sounds, as the communities compete to see whose prayer can be heard, while the organ of the Latins adds an extra element. Every time the organ quiets for silent prayer the sounds of another community take the fore, whether it be the dramatic, operatic voices of the Armenians, the Byzantine prayer of the Greeks, or the booming intonations of the Copts. The clergy produce a rainbow of color as the different communities put on their elaborately decorated vestments and crowns. The incense bearers pace around the church, the chained censers swinging to their sides as they move from altar to altar and from icon to icon in a billowing cloud of heavily scented incense.

Directly after the departure of the Latins, their carpets, patriarchal throne, and seats are quickly removed from the area in front of the Edicule, and the organ music ceases. The gate, which separates the Greek Orthodox Katholikon from the Rotunda is swung open and a Greek procession immediately takes over the space of the Rotunda, changing the liturgy in seconds from the Western to the Eastern rite. The participants all hold palm fronds in their hands as they promenade in sacramental song. A similar path is taken: around the Edicule, by the Unction Stone, thence around the ambulatory of the Katholikon, via the Altar of Mary Magdalene and back to the Katholikon, from where the patriarch returns directly through the streets to his patriarchate.

At once the triple Palm Sunday procession of the Armenians, the Copts, and the Syrians takes up position in the Rotunda. This is the first of three such processions conducted by these communities in the Holy Week. They line up around the Edicule, each church led by their *kavass*, the standard bearers, the choir and the high clergy. At the back paces the patriarch, his throne carried behind him. Again the different brocaded capes of the clergy light up the scene, the patriarchs dressed in the most striking vestments. In the hands of the participants are palm fronds and olive branches. They proceed three times around the tomb, stopping at the entrance to the Edicule where the throne is placed in position. Each patriarch conducts a short prayer ceremony, accompanied by an individual choir, before entering the tomb. The procession circumambulates the tomb, and after the third gyration the three communities return to their chapels and then depart the Church of the Holy Sepulchre.

The week days of Holy Week are marked by smaller services, usually involving limited numbers of the participants.

The Latins conduct small pilgrimages for the Monday, Tuesday, and Wednesday of Easter. The first pilgrimage is to the fifth station of the cross commemorating the site where Simon of Cyrene took the cross from Jesus. On the next day a service is held in the Chapel of the Flagellation at the far end of the Via Dolorosa, and on Wednesday the Column of the

Flagellation is exhibited in the Chapel of the Apparition. The column is decorated with flowers and a series of candelabra are placed before it while mass is celebrated in the chapel. The Orthodox churches spend these three days quietly. The Greek Orthodox pilgrims take this opportunity to visit the site of the baptism of Jesus at Kasr el-Yahud near Jericho on the Jordan River. The Armenians conduct a short mass on Tuesday of Easter at the Chapel of St. John the Less in the Parvis of the Holy Sepulchre.

Maundy Thursday and the Ceremony of the Washing of the Feet

> Jesus, knowing that the Father had given all things into his hands, and that he was come from God and went to God; He riseth from supper, laid aside his garments, and took a towel, and girded himself. After that he poureth water into a basin, and began to wash the disciples' feet, and to wipe them with the towel where with he was girded (John 13: 3–5).

His Eminence Isychios, Metropolitan of Capitolias prepares himself before the Greek Orthodox ceremony of the Washing of the Feet.

Christ's washing of his disciples' feet, in anticipation of the final episodes of his life of which he alone was then cognizant, forms the basis for one of the major events of the Jerusalem Easter. The ceremony of the Washing of the Feet, which commemorates this occasion, fully described by the Gospel of John, is observed by all the communities with great pomp and circumstance. It is to this rite that all the government and diplomatic dignitaries are invited and they sit in prominent positions to view the spectacle.

The ceremony of the Greeks is the most impressive and in good weather is conducted on a raised platform in the Parvis of the Church of the Holy Sepulchre. Early in the morning the surrounding courtyard, windows, balconies, and roofs fill up with people anxious to get a good view of the proceedings. The platform is carpeted, the patriarchal throne placed at one side flanked by two cushioned benches. On an opposite wall a number of metal loops that are orphaned for the rest of the year suddenly have significance, as a small wooden ledge is attached, with a draped reading plinth fixed facing the platform and a willow branch hung above, representing the Tree of Agony in Gethsemane. At the start of the ceremony a Greek Orthodox archimandrite climbs a ladder to this small ledge, and shortly afterwards the patriarch appears in procession with twelve further archimandrites, representing the disciples, who all climb the stairs to the central platform. The gowns of the patriarch are different for each ceremony of Easter Week, and he appears this time in a gold and silver vestment, decorated with icons and precious stones, carrying a silver scepter capped by a cross between two snakes. The archimandrites are also magnificently dressed in bright red and gold garments, but wear the usual high flat hat of the Greeks rather than the jeweled crown as worn by the patriarch. On the floor of the platform are placed a jug and a silver basin beside a bouquet of flowers. After blessing the crowd the patriarch descends from the platform and kneels in prayer to symbolize Christ's retreat from his disciples on the day prior to his trial and execution. At this time the archimandrite on the ledge begins the recitation of prayers that continues till the end of the liturgy.

The patriarch remounts the platform and his outer gown is removed to reveal a simple white robe beneath, around which a large white towel is wrapped. Water is poured into the bowl and in turn, each archimandrite removes one sock, while the patriarch kneels to wash and dry their feet. After some further prayer the patriarch removes the towel and replaces his gown and crown. The party then returns to the Greek Orthodox patriarchate in procession, the patriarch walking while dipping the flowers in the remaining water and spraying the surrounding crowd with drops of this now sanctified water.

Similar ceremonies are held by the other churches. The Latin liturgy, held within the Church of the Holy Sepulchre in front of the Edicule on the afternoon of Maundy Thursday, is a much simpler affair. Only a hundred or so participants, beside the clergy, attend the ceremony.

The Coptic Orthodox Metropolitan breaking bread during Mass in the Church of St. Anthony in the Coptic Orthodox Patriarchate on Maundy Thursday.

In fact the day has begun with the Procession of the Blessed Sacrament, which has been placed in a repository on the tomb, where it stays till Friday morning. The patriarch sits on a throne facing the tomb, with priests in two facing rows on either side. After prayer His Beatitude is dressed in a towel and the patriarch begins to wash the feet of thirteen priests and laymen who have previously removed one sock. On completion the patriarch washes his hands and reads from the Gospel of John. Immediately after the rite the Service of the Tenebrae Office is started and the doors of the church are locked for the day. At the same time a pilgrimage is made to the Upper Room, the traditional site of the Last Supper on Mount Zion, to represent the eve of Passover and another of the final events of Christ's life.

The Armenians conduct their ceremony in the Cathedral of St. James in the Armenian quarter. Dressed in elaborate brocaded garments, the ceremony is directed on the altar platform of the church, where the senior officials of the church have their feet washed by the patriarch. After washing the feet with soap, the patriarch dries them and crosses the foot with a finger dipped in olive oil.

The service of the Coptic church is in many ways the most moving. It is a private community service that takes place in the Church of St. Anthony in the Coptic Orthodox patriarchate. The people stand in a long line, starting with the clergy, the men, and finally the women of the Coptic community. His Eminence the Archbishop, the highest church official resident in Jerusalem, symbolically washes the feet of all the congregation by wiping the ankles of the devotees with a cloth dipped in sanctified water.

Good Friday

The service of the Holy Passion held on Good Friday is a central part of the Easter liturgy. It commemorates the betrayal by Judas, the arrest of Christ in Gethsemane, and his trial before Pontius Pilate at the Praetorium. The ceremonies closely follow these crucial events, from the early morning into the night.

> Then the soldiers of the governor took Jesus into the common hall [the Praetorium], and gathered unto him the whole band of soldiers. And they stripped him and put on him a scarlet robe. And when they had plaited a crown of thorns, they put it upon his head, and a reed in his right hand. And they bowed the knee before him, and mocked him, saying, "Hail, King of the Jews!" (Matthew 27:27–28).

Jesus, carrying the cross on which he was crucified, progressed along the Way of Sorrows, the Via Dolorosa, to Golgotha.

> And they took Jesus, and led him away. And he bearing his cross, went forth into a place called the place of a skull, which is called in the Hebrew Golgotha: Where they crucified him, and two others with him, on either side one, and Jesus in the midst (John 19:16–18).

After the crucifixion, Jesus was removed from the cross by Joseph of Arimathea and Nicodemus, prepared for burial and placed in a tomb.

> Then took they the body of Jesus, and wound it in linen cloths with the spices, as the manner of the Jews is to some. Now in the place where he was crucified there was a garden, and in the garden a new sepulchre, wherein was never man yet laid. There laid they Jesus therefore because of the Jews' preparation day [for Shabbat] (John 19: 40–42).

The Latin church begins the day with a procession from the Edicule, bearing the Blessed

Sacrament, which had been placed on the tomb the previous day, to Calvary, where a service is held. This is the preface for one of the most important events for the faithful of all the communities—the procession from the Praetorium, along the Via Dolorosa, past the first nine external stations of the cross, into the Church of the Holy Sepulchre. The crowds of pilgrims, local Christians, and clergy carry large wooden crosses through the streets of the Old City of Jerusalem, stopping at each station to pray and to recall the incidents which had occurred there. This is one of the few ceremonies where the lead is taken by the laity. After entering the doors of the Holy Sepulchre the cross is placed at one side and the crowd disperses, to rest before the extended evening activities. At the same time, the streets fill with new crowds, accompanied by police and a sizeable number of press photographers. Every year a group of evangelical Protestants, dressed as Roman legionaries, surround a lone devotee in a loin cloth with a crown of thorns on his head as he is tied to a cross and covered with fake blood. They march along the Via Dolorosa toward the Church of the Holy Sepulchre and they are forcibly stopped, every year, by the police before they can enter the Parvis.

A scene from the Latin procession from the Praetorium along the Via Dolorosa.

The afternoon and evening are devoted to the burial service of Christ, which is conducted in the church in turn by each community, except for the Armenian Orthodox, who conduct the rite in their Cathedral of St. James. The most graphic of the services is celebrated by the Latins, represented this time by the Franciscan Custos of the Holy Land. After the faithful have passed through the first nine stations of the cross during the day, the last five stations, all located within the church, are visited during the burial service. A wooden statue of Christ is carried behind a cross from the Franciscan Chapel of the Apparition, to the tenth station of the cross—the Prison of Christ, which is located in the northern transept. The faithful then visit and pray at the shrines in the ambulatory that represent the final events of Jesus's life, beginning with the Chapel of St. Longinus, the centurion who stabbed the body of Jesus to show he was dead.

> [...]when they came to Jesus, and saw that he was dead already, they brake not his legs [to hasten death]: But one of the soldiers with a spear pierced his side, and forthwith came there out blood and water (John 19: 33–34).

The procession then moves to the Chapel of the Parting of the Raiment, which commemorates the distribution of Jesus's clothing by lot amongst the soldiers, and thence to the Chapel of the Crowning of the Thorns or the Derision of Christ, which commemorates the placing of thorns on Christ's head prior to his execution and the mocking to which he was subjected in his passage through the streets of Jerusalem.

The statue of Christ is then taken up to Calvary where it is attached to the wooden cross for a symbolic crucifixion. After the statue is lowered from the cross in solemn prayer the metaphorical Christ is borne from Golgotha to the Unction Stone, where the body is cleaned, anointed, and wrapped in a white linen shroud. The Franciscan friars then carry the enshrouded statue to the Edicule, where it is laid on the burial slab and the tomb is sealed.

The Orthodox churches also conduct solemn burial processions on the same route, bearing a graphic representation of Christ painted or embroidered on a piece of cloth. This banner, covered with flower petals, is carried by four senior clergy around the Edicule, and later placed in the tomb prior to sealing. Lamentation prayers are chanted throughout the service. The burial procession for the Greek Orthodox takes place twice: once, in parade around the Parvis, for the local Christians, and then, a little later at night, for the Greek church. For the pilgrims from Greece, the Mediterranean Islands and Russia this marks the preparation for the celebration of the Holy Fire. The pilgrims fill every space in the church, spreading blankets and folding chairs over the floors. Soon the Rotunda is filled, and the *kavass* push and shove in order to make way for the procession. At the end of the service the pilgrims attempt to

A Coptic altar boy.

ensure themselves a good seat for the next day. At midnight, after the Greek Orthodox clergy have left, the police drive the disappointed devotees out of the church into the Parvis. The floor is then superficially cleaned and the space around the Edicule is partitioned with steel barriers between the Armenians, the Syrian Orthodox, the Copts, and the local Greek Orthodox Christians, leaving space for the foreign Orthodox only within the Katholikon. At this stage the doors of the Church of the Holy Sepulchre are sealed.

Holy Saturday and the Ceremony of the Holy Fire

Forming the climax of Holy Week of the Orthodox Easter is the famous Holy Fire ceremony, which is unique to the Church of the Holy Sepulchre.

> [...]the crowd waited in the rotunda, chanting "Kyrie Eleison," each one searching the innermost depths of his soul, thinks of his sins, and says secretly to himself, "Will my sins prevent the descent of the Holy Light?" At the end of the ninth hour [...] the Holy Light suddenly illuminated the Holy Sepulchre, shining with an awe inspiring and splendid brightness [...] Man can experience no joy like that which every Christian feels at the moment when he sees the Holy Light of God. He who has not taken part in the glory of that day will not believe the record of all that I have seen (Abbot Daniel, A.D. 1106–7).

Indeed, to this day, the ceremony is unlike any other, and its origin mysterious. The ceremony symbolizes the resurrection of Christ, as represented by the miracle of light that descends from the heavens to rekindle the lamp that hangs in the Holy Sepulchre, extinguished on Good Friday. Though the Orthodox clergy take pains to explain that the Holy Fire is no miracle, it is seen as such by the people and it creates scenes of devotional hysteria unlike any other in Holy Week.

The solemn opening of the door of the church is conducted by the Armenian dragoman at 8:00 a.m. At once the crowds of local Christians, who have been waiting in the Parvis, stream in to take their places, the clergy making sure that only members of the appropriate congregations end up in their predesignated positions. The Armenians occupy the areas south of the Edicule, beside their gallery; the Copts — behind the tomb, beside their chapel; the Syrian Orthodox — to the north of the entrance to the Chapel of Nicodemus; and finally the Arab Orthodox to the north of the Edicule. All hold tapers and candles that will later be lit from the Holy Fire. Other pilgrims are allowed to enter the Katholikon and the ambulatory behind it. Soon the Rotunda fills with loud voices as the different communities try to outshout each other with religious chants. The Russian and Greek pilgrims, most of them middle-aged women dressed entirely in black, fervently cross themselves in a remarkable display of religious ardor.

The Armenian patriarch enters at 10:30, conducts a single circuit around the tomb and then climbs up to his throne in the gallery above the tomb, from where he will observe the scene.

At 11:00 a large block of wax is taken by a Greek priest to the Edicule. The interior of the tomb is searched for any matches or other fire-lighting materials, and the tomb is sealed with the wax jointly by Greek, Armenian, and Syrian priests and one of the Muslim guardians of the tomb. A Franciscan monk, the only representative of his community, stands at one side, while the doors and gallery of the Latin sections of the church often staying dark, locked, and empty, expressing the disapproval of that church of the proceedings.

Then the local Christian youth march in from around the Old City, men carried on the shoulders of others, into the passage around the Rotunda where they parade, gesticulate, clap, and excite the members of their congregation, raising the emotions of the spectators to a fever pitch. Meanwhile the Greek Orthodox patriarch goes down the internal staircase of the patriarchate directly to the Parvis, where he is checked about his person to verify that no lighting materials are hidden in his vestments. He then proceeds directly to his throne in the Katholikon.

Following the entry of His Beatitude the Greek Orthodox patriarch, the Coptic and Syrian Orthodox clergy, who have entered the church for prayer in the early morning, proceed to the Armenian vestry where they call on the Armenian patriarch and present him with their bundles of Holy Fire candles. Then, together with him, they continue to the Katholikon, where they pay their joint respects to the Greek Orthodox patriarch, to whom they hand the candle bundles, and the three community heads return to their places. Now the Greek Guardian of the Holy Sepulchre, accompanied by the dragoman, takes the quenched lamp of the church from the treasury beside the Unction Stone to the Edicule, where it will later be rekindled by the Holy Spirit.

With an outburst of bells the doors of the Katholikon are swung open and a procession of Greek priests, robed in white and gold and preceded by bearers of banners and incense, exits to parade thrice around the tomb. At the end of the parade paces the patriarch, dressed in his jewels of office and wearing his crown. After the third revolution the patriarch is relieved of his outer robe and crown. The seals of the Edicule are broken and, together with an Armenian prelate, the patriarch enters the Tomb of Christ and the doors close behind them. In anticipation, the crowd falls silent, the church bells ring out and after a few minutes of suspense a flash of flame is seen from within the tomb. A cluster of lighted candles is thrust first through an opening in the south side of the Edicule to a layman of the Armenian community, who runs up to the gallery to present it to the Armenian patriarch. Coptic and Syrian laymen then carry their blazing candle-bundles from the same opening to their communities and chapels. At the same time another bunch of candles is handed through the northern opening of the Edicule to a parish priest who takes it to the Guardian of the Holy Sepulchre in the Katholikon. Amidst wild excitement the doors of the tomb are flung open and the Greek patriarch appears with two huge bundles of candles and is held aloft. People then start to light their own candles from the central source, and flames and clouds of smoke soon fill the church while the devotees repeatedly cross themselves. Runners carry lighted candles to the many pilgrims who fill the Parvis, the dome above the Edicule, and the roof. Soon these areas are also ablaze with myriad lights.

Immediately the Greek Orthodox patriarch exits the basilica and a tripartite procession, with the participation of the Armenians, the Copts, and the Syrians, encircles the Holy Sepulchre three times. In front pace the bearers of banners, incense, candles, crosses, and bibles, followed by the bishops who in turn stop in front of the tomb for prayer.

The most important ceremony of the Ethiopian Orthodox church is held later that evening on the roof of the Chapel of St. Helena. It is easy to imagine that one is in Africa, as the area of Deir es-Sultan is crowded with white clothed pilgrims from Ethiopia. Out of a tent appears the Ethiopian patriarch, proceeded by a huge drum and dancers. He holds a large candle from which the pilgrims light their own tapers, as he proceeds thrice around the dome of the chapel, lighting up the night with flames. Soon after, the closing events of Easter in the Church of the Holy Sepulchre commence, as devotees gather for Midnight Mass.

Easter Sunday

In the end of the Sabbath, as it began to dawn toward the first day of the week, came Mary Magdalene and the other Mary to see the sepulchre. And behold, there was a great earthquake; for the angel of the Lord descended from heaven and came and rolled back the stone from the door, and sat upon it [...] the angel [said to] the women, "Fear not ye; for I know that ye seek Jesus which was crucified. He is not here; for he is risen, as he said" (Matthew 28: 1–6).

Just before midnight the Latins gather in front of the Edicule and then move to the Chapel of St.

His Beatitude Diodorus I, the Greek Orthodox Patriarch of Jerusalem, clutching bundles of candles lit from the Holy Fire, is carried from the Edicule to the Katholikon.

Oil lamps blaze above the tomb of Christ. Each oil lamp is marked with the symbol of the community to which it belongs. These are the property of the Franciscan Custody of the Holy Land.

Mary Magdalene, the Chapel of the Apparition, and Calvary for a series of masses conducted by His Paternity the Custos of Terra Sancta, in which the resurrection of Christ is celebrated.

Similarly at midnight the Greek Mass of the Resurrection begins with yet another procession, featuring the Greek Orthodox patriarch dressed in white. After circumambulating the tomb three times in prayer, the patriarch enters the tomb to find it empty. Exiting the Holy Sepulchre he raises his arms and proclaims:

"Christ is risen! Alleluia! Alleluia! He is risen indeed!"

With this the bells clash, the banners and candles are raised and lowered and the pilgrims, who are by now truly excited, chant "Christ has Risen!" over and over. Holy Communion is served, first by two senior metropolitans to the patriarch himself, and then by the patriarch to the metropolitans, who reverently kiss his hand. This marks the beginning of commotion as the Sacrament is handed out to the faithful before they make their way home through the almost empty streets of the Old City of Jerusalem, as yet another procession of the Armenians, Copts, and Syrians forms around the tomb and continues into the early light of Easter morning.

The City and the Church

Previous pages: The dome above the Katholikon, the Greek Orthodox chapel lying at the center of the Church of the Holy Sepulchre, rises over the roof of the Ambulatory. The dome was rebuilt by the Greek architect Nikolaos Komnenos in 1809-10 to replace that destroyed by the disastrous fire in 1808.
Below: The two domes of the Church of the Holy Sepulchre are one of the dominant features above the roofs of the Old City of Jerusalem. In the foreground, the belfry can be seen.

Under the spring almond blossom vendors fill the streets of the "Muristan" to the east of the Church of the Holy Sepulchre. Police barriers mark the path of pilgrims who walk along the Via Dolorosa, via the Muristan to the Church. The Muristan is the site of the buildings associated with the Hospitaller Order founded in the 12th century and existing to this day.

A column set to the left of the main entrance to the Church of the Holy Sepulchre is engraved with crosses left by centuries of pilgrimage. In the crack that runs the length of the column a pilgrim has placed a note asking for a blessing at this important shrine.

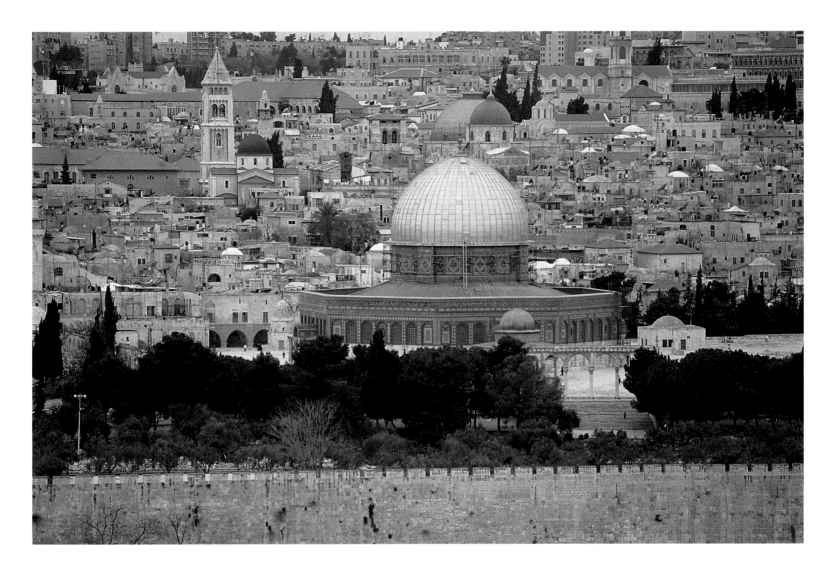

This is probably the most famous view of Jerusalem from the Mount of Olives to the west, overlooking the Temple Mount into the Old City. Above the wall of the Temple Mount, which existed at the time of Jesus, is the Dome of the Rock, almost certainly located on the site of the Temple and now marking the site of the ascension of Muhammad. Beyond this are the domes and belfry of the Church of the Holy Sepulchre. To its left is the tower of the Lutheran Church of the Redeemer, built on the site of the Hospitaller church of St. Maria Latina in the Muristan.

Icons, postcards, glitzy 3-D pictures, crucifixes, trinkets and even tins of Holy Land air are the fare offered to modern pilgrims. This trade, which is as ancient as the church, once offered "genuine" pieces of the True Cross, relics, and models of the Church of the Holy Sepulchre.

The facade of the Church of the Holy Sepulchre, built in the twelfth century, is one of the outstanding achievements of Crusader art and architecture in the Holy Land. Above its double portal were set two decorative lintels, one describing events from the life of Christ, and the other decorated with a vegetative and figurative relief. The disintegrating lintels were removed in 1929 and are displayed in the Rockefeller Museum.

The belfry of the church, originally constructed by the Crusaders, rises above a secluded garden within the Gethsemane Monastery, located opposite the Church of the Holy Sepulchre. Earthquakes and time have dislodged the upper three stories of the tower leaving an unsatisfying stump. Flying above it the flag of the Greek Orthodox Patriarchate of Jerusalem displays their control of the belfry and most of its internal spaces in accordance with the 1852 Status Quo agreement between the different ecclesiastical communities. Following pages: A nocturnal photograph of the eastern side of the Church of the Holy Sepulchre shows the Katholikon dome and the roof over the Ambulatory. To the left is the minaret of the Mosque of Omar, built by Saladin at the entrance of the Church, after he reconquered the city for Islam from the Crusader Kingdom of Jerusalem in 1187 A.D.

The Opening of the Doors

Previous pages: The great wooden doors of the Church of the Holy Sepulchre are scarred with history. Worth noting are the ancient padlock and the closed hatch through which the ladder is passed to the gatekeeper so that he can unlock the church. The doors are locked most nights 15 minutes after the sunset, except during festivals. Clergy of the different communities stay inside throughout the night in order to protect their denominational interests and property. The story of the doors, keys and doorkeepers of the Church of the Holy Sepulchre is the stuff of an epic saga in itself.

As the Church of the Holy Sepulchre is the joint property of a number of Christian communities, the possession of the key, once a bone of contention, is today defined by the Status Quo agreement. After the expulsion of the Crusaders, entrance was restricted by the Muslim rulers, and before the rule of Ibrahim Pasha, access was permitted only on the payment of a fee. Until 1831 the key was owned by the Muslim Joudeh family, while the day-to-day opening of the door was entrusted then as now with members of the Nusseibeh family. Here a member of the Franciscan Custody of the Holy Land waits, key in hand, outside the Church before the Solemn Opening of the doors.

*Metropolitan Daniel of Mount Tabor, the
Greek Orthodox Superior of the Church
of the Holy Sepulchre, stands like a sentry
at the closed door of the Church awaiting
one of the three solemn openings of the
doors conducted once each by Latins (on
Palm Sunday), Greeks (on Good Friday)
and Armenians (on Holy Saturday)
during the Easter Holy week. The
conduct and sequence of events of the
solemn entry are strictly codified.*

After having been closed inside the church all night, a pilgrim awaits the solemn opening of the doors. The ladder, used to reach the padlock, is propped up beside the hatch.

During the Latin solemn entry on Palm Sunday the Latin Sacristan inside passes the ladder through the hatch to the waiting gatekeeper outside watched by representatives of the Latin Patriarchate and the Franciscan Custody of the Holy Land, who have guarded Catholic interests in the Church of the Holy Sepulchre since the 14th century.

The Muslim gatekeeper, a member of one of the two families entrusted with the opening of the doors of the church since the Middle Ages, climbs the ladder to unlock the ancient padlock.

After the Greek Orthodox solemn opening of the Church of the Holy Sepulchre on Good Friday, conducted by the Chief Dragoman, Metropolitan Christodoulos of Eleftheropolis, the two door wings are swung open and the crowd surges in.
Upon unlocking the padlocks the first door wing is pulled open by the Sacristan inside the Church of the Holy Sepulchre. The second wing is then pushed open by the Muslim gatekeeper from the outside.

The Greek Orthodox

Previous pages: A Russian Orthodox monk prays by candlelight in a corner of the Church of the Holy Sepulchre. The Russian Orthodox are associated with the Greek Orthodox and were their major protectors during Ottoman rule in the 19th century, donating much of the money for the 1808 reconstruction of the Tomb of Christ, the Edicule.

The Greek Orthodox Chapel of the Raising of the Cross, on Golgotha or Calvary, is located on the traditional site of the crucifixion of Jesus. The exact spot is preserved under the altar covered by glass. To the right of the chapel is the Latin altar of Our Lady of Sorrows or Stabat Mater, commemorating the place where the Virgin Mary grieved upon receiving the body of Jesus after it was taken down from the cross. The bust was presented to the Church of the Holy Sepulchre by Portugal in 1778.

His Eminence Vassilius Senior Metropolitan of Caesarea officiates Mass for the Greek Orthodox community.

The Greek Orthodox Superior of the Church of the Holy Sepulchre, Metropolitan Daniel, observes from a side bench the ceremony of one of the other communities, to verify that none of the rights of his own church are encroached upon.

Pilgrims from the Greek Islands, typically dressed entirely in black, hold candles and pray before lighting them for benediction. They place the candles in sand trays along the walls of the Edicule.

Carrying an icon of Jesus riding a white ass into Jerusalem as the Messiah and holding a palm frond, two members of the Greek Orthodox Brotherhood of the Church of the Holy Sepulchre participate in the Palm Procession from Bet Phage via the Mount of Olives to the Old City of Jerusalem. The Greek Orthodox procession takes place on Lazarus Saturday, the day before Palm Sunday.

On Palm Sunday a pilgrim, holding a palm frond, patiently awaits the procession to reach her as it enters the Church of the Holy Sepulchre from the Greek Orthodox Patriarchate. Following pages: Representing His Beatitude the Greek Orthodox Patriarch of Jerusalem, Diodorus I, His Eminence Benedictos Archibishop of Gaza officiates over the Good Friday procession in front of the Tomb of Christ. Note the colorfully embroided robe, the jewelled crown and the staff topped with two vipers.

His Eminence Isychios, Metropolitan of Capitolias, representing the Patriarch of Jerusalem, proceeds from the Church of the Holy Sepulchre to the Parvis for the ceremony of the Washing of the Feet on the morning of Maundy Thursday. This ceremony commemorates the washing of the apostles' feet by Jesus at the Last Supper as recounted in the Gospel of John. It is conducted by the head of every community.

Before proceeding with the ceremony of the Washing of the Feet, His Eminence Isychios Metropolitan of Capitolias is derobed of his heavily embroided gown by archimandrites of the Brotherhood of the Church of the Holy Sepulchre. Before him, on a carpet woven with the symbol of the Patriarchate of Jerusalem, is a silver bowl and ewer with which he will wash the feet of twelve archimandrites representing the twelve apostles.

Set in the floor of the Katholikon is a marble dais called the "compas." By tradition this is the center or "omphalos" (navel) of the world which appears in many medieval maps, illustrations and models of the Church of the Holy Sepulchre. Here pilgrims place candles for blessings on a stand at its side.

Each with a candle in hand, Greek clergy circumambulate the Edicule during one of the three Easter processions deported around the Tomb of Christ by every community during Easter Holy Week.

His Eminence Vassilios, Senior Metropolitan of Caesarea and His Eminence Constantine, Senior Metropolitan of Scythopolis line the Katholikon, candle in hand, during the Lithurgy of the Resurrection between Holy Saturday and Easter Sunday.

Standing with his back to the "compas," the traditional center of the world,
a member of the Brotherhood of the Church of the Holy Sepulchre passes
between two rows of Metropolitans and Archbishops of the Greek
Orthodox Patriarchate toward the iconostasis of the Katholikon.

An icon of the Madonna and Child in the Greek Orthodox Chapel of St. James the Less.

High above the floor of the Katholikon huge pilasters support the smaller of the two domes of the Church of the Holy Sepulchre. Though the columns and the dome were originally built in the Crusader period, the decoration has only recently been completed in colored mosaic. The composition is a common theme of Orthodox iconography showing Christ holding the Bible as ruler of the world (Christ Pantocrator) surrounded by the apostles and archangels.

In an underground chamber of the St. Abraham Convent, to the east of the Parvis, is the now disused dining room (refectorium). Its walls are decorated with paintings that cover all its surfaces showing Christ, biblical figures, apostles, archangels, hermits, and saints. At the two ends of the chamber are paintings of the Last Supper and of the Passage of Mary to Bethlehem. These murals probably date to the 19th century.

Cherubs occupy the apex of the chamber, representing the heavens.

On a panel at one end of the room is a representation of King David flanked by the High Priest Aharon and the prophet Elijah.

At the center of the vault is the image of Christ Pantocrator, set above three cherubs with angels to his side emphasizing his celestial abode.

The Latins

Previous pages: Candle flares mark the path of the Easter procession of the Latins from the Chapel of St. Mary Magdalene, in the Latin section on the northern aisle of the Church of the Holy Sepulchre, past the front of the Edicule, on to the Unction Stone in the entrance hall.

Catholic pilgrims from all over the world participate in the Palm Sunday procession from Bet Phage on the Mount of Olives to St. Anne's Convent beside the Lions or St. Stephen's Gate of the Old City. The pilgrims recite prayers and carry olive branches and palm fronds to commemorate the entry of Jesus into the city of Jerusalem.

His Beatitude Monsignor Michel Sabbah the Latin Patriarch of Jerusalem, His Eminence Bishop Kamal – Hanna Bathish the Vicar General of the
Latin Patriarch of Jerusalem and the Most Reverend Father Giovanni Battistelli OFM, the Custos of the Holy Land walk with the Latin clergy,
Catholic Officials and Franciscan friars at the back of the Palm Sunday procession. Flanking them are rows of deacons and local Catholic scouts.
At the back can be seen members of the Equestrian Order of the Church of the Holy Sepulchre in black felt berets.

The Palm Sunday procession descends the steep slope of the Mount of Olives, between the walls of the Jewish cemetery and the Church of Dominus Flevit, whose name commemorates the mourning by Jesus following his premonition of the destruction of Jerusalem as described in Luke. In the background is the Muslim shrine known as the Dome of the Rock, the traditional site of the ascension of Muhammad and before that the location of the Jewish Temple.

After the Palm Sunday procession reaches the Lions or St. Stephen's Gate, the bagpipe bands of the Catholic scouts march through the streets of Jerusalem to the Latin Patriarchate inside the New Gate.

Franciscan friars, in ceremonial cassocks, wait in line during the Blessing of the Palms by the Latin Patriarch in the Church of the Holy Sepulchre on Palm Sunday.

On the Wednesday of Holy Week the Column of the Flagellation is dressed with decorations in an alcove in the Chapel of the Apparition, in the northern part of the Church of the Holy Sepulchre. The column is by tradition part of the column to which Jesus was tied and whipped after his trial by Pontius Pilate. Another column also associated with this event is displayed on an altar in the Armenian gallery chapel.

To the side of the entrance into the Chapel of the Angel in the Edicule are the huge candlesticks belonging to the three major communities, the Greek Orthodox, the Latins, and the Armenians. Around them are flowers that are placed there only during the Easter services.

On Good Friday the local Catholic lay community walk in procession the length of Via Dolorosa, the Street of Sorrows, carrying a huge wooden cross from the Praetorium via the nine external Stations of the Cross to the Church of the Holy Sepulchre where the pilgrims visit Calvary and the Edicule.

A nun at prayer.

His Beatitude Monsignor Michel Sabbah the Latin Patriarch of Jerusalem, sits on a temporary throne before the Edicule for Easter Mass.

The Rotunda is filled with the Good Friday procession which circumambulates the Edicule. At the back, the figurine of Christ covered by a shroud is symbolically buried after three turns of the Edicule.

Franciscan friars dressed in white ceremonial cassocks meander from the Latin Chapel of St. Mary Magdalene into the Rotunda for Mass in front of the Edicule.

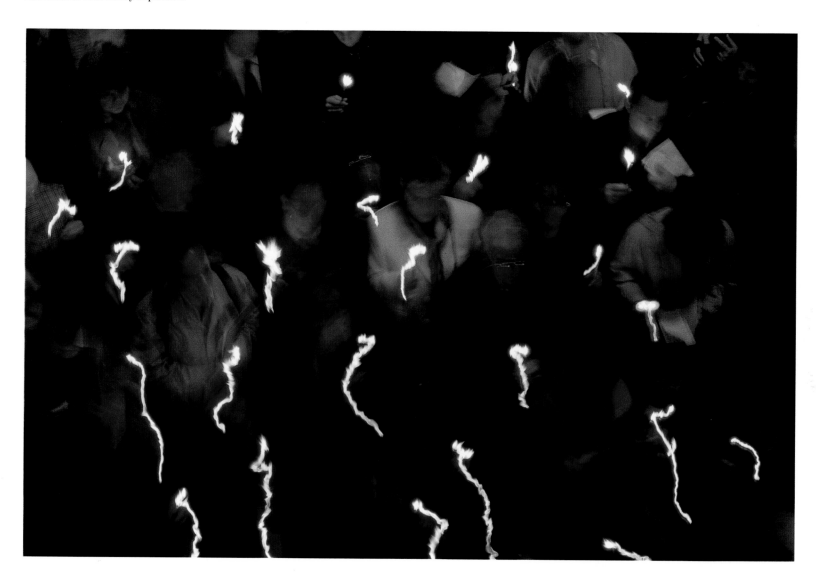

Catholic pilgrims at prayer during the Burial Service on Good Friday.

On Holy Saturday the Baptismal Font is blessed in a service in the northern part of the Rotunda. In the picture one can see the gold and silver baptismal ewer and font laid on a temporary altar during the service officiated by the Latin Patriarch of Jerusalem.

The Armenians

Previous pages: On the Tuesday of Holy Week, the Armenian Church spreads a carpet for Mass in the Parvis before the Armenian Chapel of St. James. Here a deacon, surrounded by choirboys, reads from the Gospel. At the back stand members of the Brotherhood of St. James, whose 50 members run the Armenian Patriarchate of Jerusalem.

At the end of the Palm Sunday procession within the Church of the Holy Sepulchre, deacons, carrying olive branches and palm fronds lead the Armenian procession out of the church through the streets back to the Patriarchate in the southwest section of the Old City.

The Armenian Patriarchal Vicar leads the Palm Sunday procession around the Edicule, which is conducted together with the Coptic and Syrian Orthodox Churches. Note the incredibly elaborate embroidery of the mitre and cape which are used once a year on this occasion.

Armenian Bishops and members of the Brotherhood of St. James in magnificent robes stand with their backs to the Edicule giving benediction during the Palm Sunday procession around the Edicule. Each holds a palm frond, a cross formed from a palm leaf and a candle.

An Armenian clergyman reads from the Gospels at Mass in the Parvis on the Tuesday of Easter.
Below, the Armenian Sacristan leads prayer during the service in front of the Armenian Chapel of St. James.

From a window above the Church's main portals, two Armenian priests view the Greek ceremony of the Washing of the Feet that takes place in the Parvis of the Church of the Holy Sepulchre. One priest rests his foot on the famous ladder set in position prior to the 1852 Status Quo agreements, the constraints of which allow nothing to be moved in areas of joint ownership without the agreement of the three leading church communities.

Ceremonial staffs fringed with bells.
Next page: Posed like still-life statues covered in drapes,
Armenian clergy capped with pointed cloth scarfs, form
almost abstract shapes during Mass in the Parvis.

His Beatitude Torkum Manoogian, the Armenian Patriarch of Jerusalem, washes the feet of one of his bishops during the ceremony of the Washing of the Feet in the Cathedral of St. James in the Armenian Patriarchate.

On Easter Sunday, at six o'clock in the morning, after a night of prayer and processions, a three-hour long High Mass is held in front of the Tomb of Christ to celebrate the Resurrection.

After the ceremony of the Washing of the Feet on Maundy Thursday, the Armenian Patriarch of Jerusalem in a bejeweled crown, the Patriarchal Vicar with a shepherd's crook and a mitre, and the Bishops of the Brotherhood of St. James all stand in front of the altar and face their congregation for a final blessing before dispersal.

The Copts

Previous pages: During the Burial Procession on Good Friday, His Eminence Archbishop Dr. Anba Abraham, the Coptic Orthodox Metropolitan of Jerusalem and the Near East blesses the Unction Stone together with the clergy of his church. At either side of the stone are three candlesticks of the three major communities, and above the stone are lanterns also belonging to these three communities. The lighting of the candles and lanterns is strictly controlled by the Status Quo accord.

Opposite: The Coptic Orthodox Patriarchate is located to the north of the Church of the Holy Sepulchre. The main building, the entrance of which is shown here, was constructed in the 19th century over earlier remains.

Above: Beside the Patriarchate is the 19th century Cathedral of St. Antony, built directly upon a Crusader hall that formed part of the complex added to the Church of the Holy Sepulchre in the 12th century.

The Coptic Orthodox Metropolitan of Jerusalem, carrying a palm frond,
leaves his Patriarchate and walks to the Church of the Holy Sepulchre,
where he will be dressed in ceremonial garments for the Palm Sunday
service beside the Coptic Chapel located behind the Edicule.

A Coptic monk holds a cross on Easter Sunday.

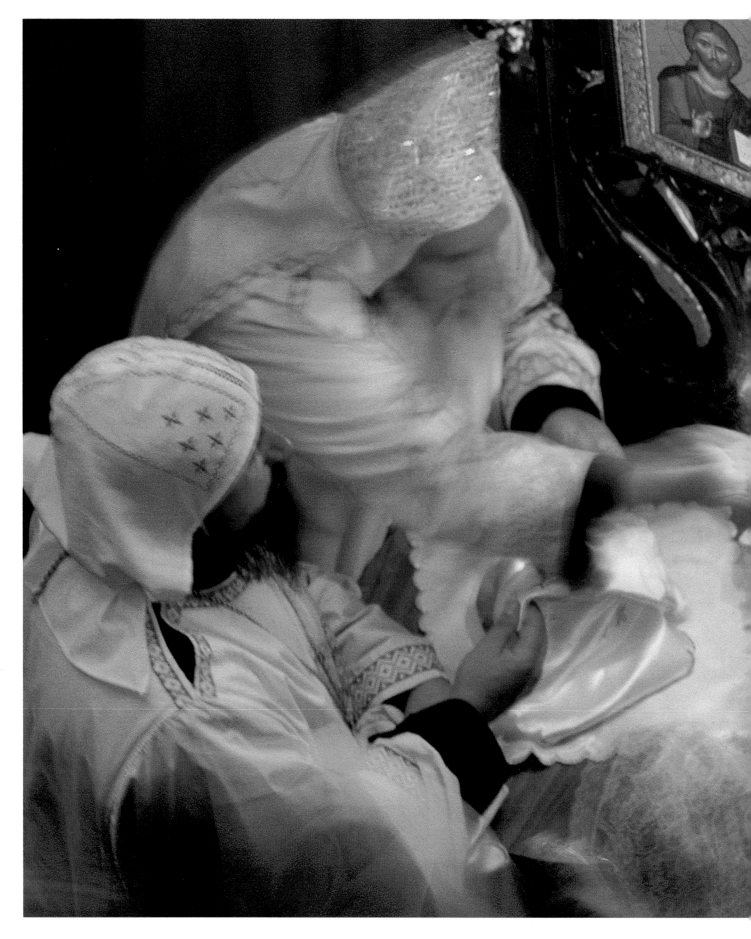

In a moving egalitarian ceremony, His Eminence Archbishop Dr. Anba Abraham, the Coptic Orthodox Metropolitan of Jerusalem and the Near East, dressed in white robes with gold embroidery, anoints the feet of his entire community during the ceremony of the Washing of the Feet on Maundy Thursday in the Cathedral of St. Anthony.

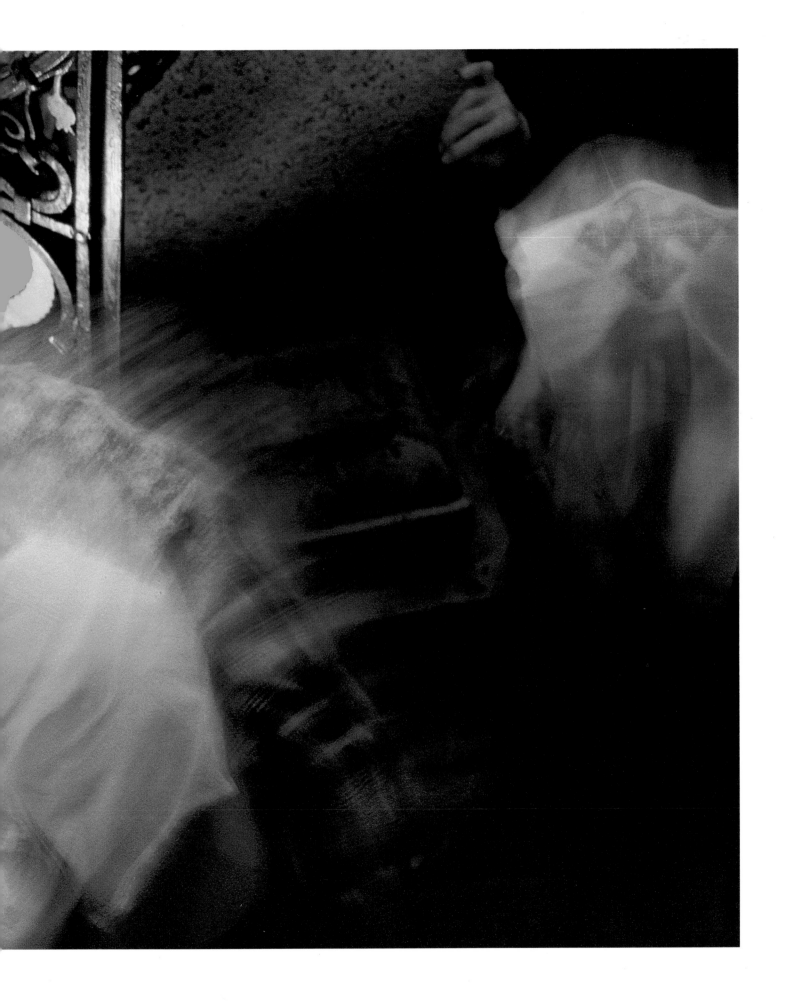

The Coptic Orthodox Metropolitan of Jerusalem wearing his ceremonial crown covered with jewels and icons.

For every procession there is a different robe. Here Archbishop Dr. Anba Abraham circles the Edicule carrying a staff topped by two vipers.

During the Burial Procession on Good Friday the Coptic clergy visit all the important sites in the Church of the Holy Sepulchre. Here the Coptic Metropoliatn prays before the Greek Orthodox shrine on Golgotha. A Greek Orthodox priest stands nearby to safeguard the interests of his church.

The Coptic Chapel is set at the back of the Edicule where a small segment of the tomb is exposed. On Palm Sunday the Jerusalem Coptic congregation gathers beside their chapel before the arrival of the procession.

Previous pages: Facing the entrance of the Chapel of the Angel in the Edicule, surrounded by his clergy, His Eminence Mar Swerios Malki Murad, Syrian Orthodox Metropolitan and Patriarchal Vicar of Jerusalem, Jordan, and the Holy Land, reads a prayer during the procession that circumambulates the Edicule after the ceremony of the Holy Fire.

The Syrian Orthodox Church is the smallest of the communities with prayer rights in the Church of the Holy Sepulchre. Here can be seen the entrance of the Syrian Orthodox Patriarchate located in the Armenian Quarter dedicated to St. Mark. It was built within a 12th century church, which according to Syrian tradition is set at the site of the Last Supper.

Above: Prior to the ceremony of the Washing of the Feet the Syrian Archbishop reads from the Gospel of St. John in Aramaic, the ancient Semitic language used in Judaea during the time of Jesus.

Opposite: Twelve members of the Syrian Orthodox lay community, representing the apostles, wait in turn to have their feet washed by the Metropolitan during the ceremony of the Washing of the Feet on Maundy Thursday. It is considered to be a great honor to be chosen to participate and family members undulate from the gallery during the rites.

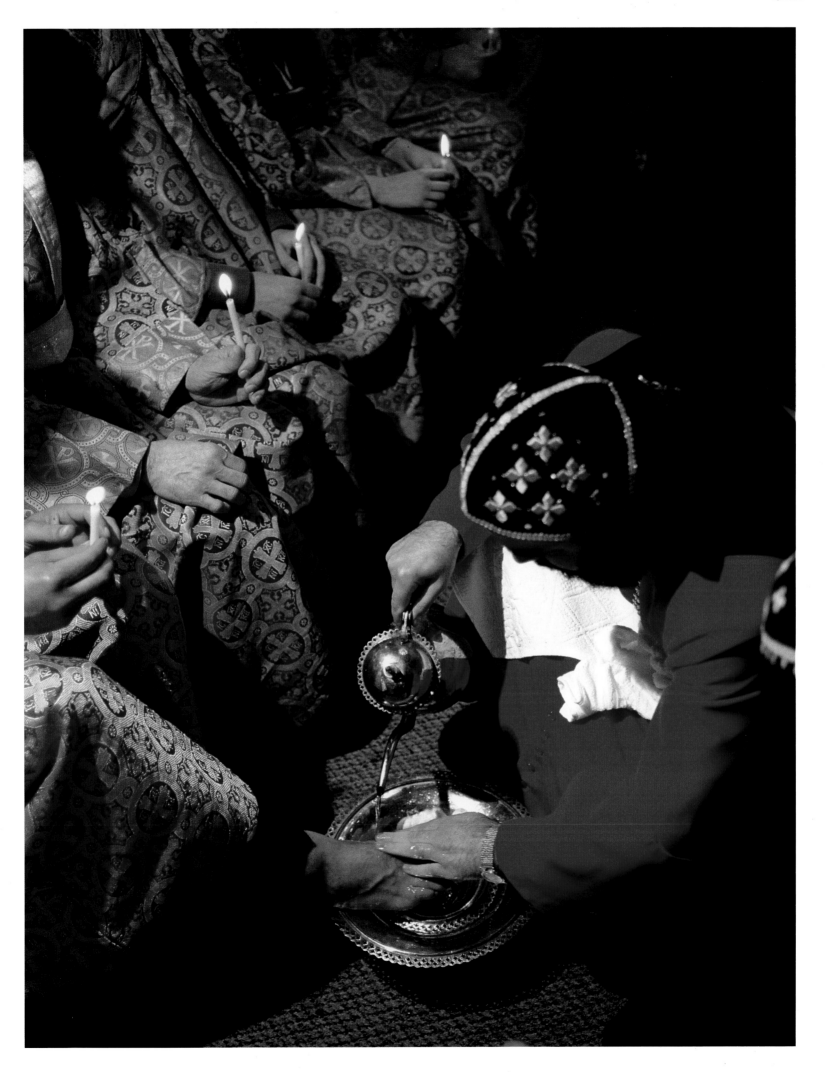

In a crumbling alcove at the back of the Rotunda in the Church of the Holy Sepulchre, the Syrian Orthodox Metropolitan holds Mass for his congregants who can hardly squeeze into the tiny space available to them. The room is the cause of a long-standing territorial dispute between the Syrian and Armenian communities.

After the Palm Sunday procession inside the Church of the Holy Sepulchre, the Syrian Orthodox Metropolitan, after removing his ceremonial gown, walks back through the Parvis on his way to the Patriarchate.

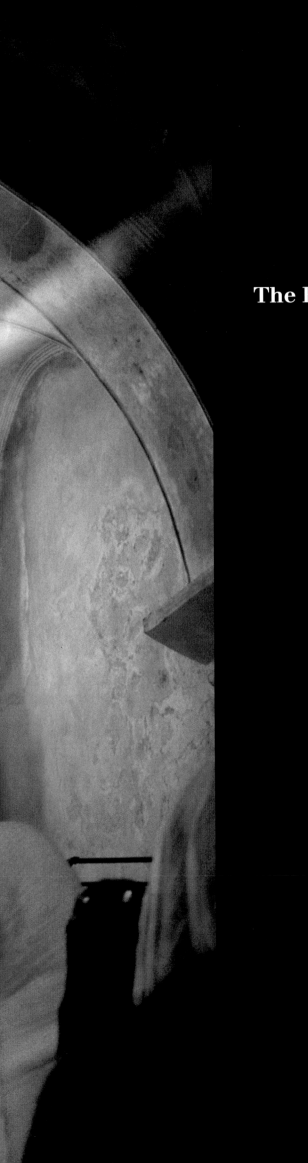

The Ethiopians

Previous pages: White-clad pilgrims conduct prayers in Geez, an ancient Ethiopian language, during Good Friday, in the Crusader Chapel of St. Michael, claimed both by the Ethiopians and the Coptic church.

An Ethiopian monk stands beside the cupola of the Chapel of St. Helena.

At the center of the courtyard of Deir es-Sultan is the cupola of the Armenian Chapel of St. Helena. The courtyard is all that remains of the now destroyed Crusader cloister of the Augustinian priory. Behind the cupola is the roof of the Ambulatory of the Church of the Holy Sepulchre and the dome above the Katholikon.

The Ethiopian Orthodox Church is restricted to an area known as Deir es-Sultan on the roof of St. Helena's Chapel.

A lone pilgrim stands in solitary prayer in the Parvis, beside the door of the Chapel of St. Michael. Beside her are wooden crosses abandoned by other pilgrims, who carry them the length of the Via Dolorosa before leaving them below the Chapel of the Agony of the Virgin.

Ethiopian pilgrims.

An Ethiopian pilgrim prays beside a gap in the canvas after finding no room in the crowded Easter tent.

A file of Ethiopian pilgrims, covered in white apparel, enter the roof area from the door beside the ninth Station of the Cross, on their way to the Ethiopian Chapel of St. Michael.

*Pilgrims seated on the pavement
of Deir es-Sultan during the Holy
Fire Ceremony.*

The major event of the Ethiopian
Orthodox Easter calender is
conducted on Holy Saturday, in the
evening following the Holy Fire
ceremony. A candle lit from the
miraculous Holy Fire is kept ablaze
until the ceremony. The Ethiopian
Archbishop leads prayers in a tent
raised on the Deir es-Sultan roof
and then heads a torchlight
procession of his clergy three times
around the cupola of the St. Helena
Chapel. Their tapers are ignited
from the Holy Fire candle held by
the Archbishop. He is accompanied
by a band of African drummers
and dancers who add special color
to the occasion, again showing
how each community expresses
its own cultural traditions in
the conduct of religious rites.

The faces of Ethiopian pilgrims are illuminated by candles during the Holy Fire procession on Holy Saturday.

Following pages: The Head of the Ethiopian Orthodox Church in Jerusalem, His Eminence Archbishop Matthewos, leads Mass before his community in a tent erected in Deir es-Sultan before the ceremony of the Washing of the Feet.

The Holy Fire Ceremony

Previous pages: Moments after the ignition of the Holy Fire the Rotunda is ablaze with the candles of the devotees who surround the Tomb of Christ, from within which the miraculous fire has sprung forth, to fill every available space in the church with flames and billowing smoke.

In the hour prior to the ceremony of the Holy Fire commences, the local Christian communities fill previously designated spaces around the Edicule. The youths beat tambours, dance, and shout slogans in a sometimes not too good-humored intercommunity rivalry.

High in the dome of the Rotunda, pilgrims await the miracle of the Holy Fire.

The devotees pass from candle to candle the Holy Fire which was originally ignited in the Tomb of Christ from the bunch of tapers presented to the assembled crowd by the Greek Orthodox Patriarch. The Rotunda quickly fills with flame, the smell of burning wax, and a cloud of thick smoke.

A layman of the Armenian community reaches into the opening on the southern face of the Edicule to take a burning bunch of candles from an Armenian Prelate who accompanies the Greek Orthodox Patriarch into the tomb. The candles, lit from the Holy Fire, are then rushed up to the Armenian Patriarch of Jerusalem, waiting in the Rotunda gallery above the Tomb of Christ.

Surrounded by devotees, His Beatitude the Greek Orthodox Patriarch of Jerusalem, Diodorus I emerges from the Edicule after lighting the Holy Fire.

Selected Bibliography

Biddle, Martin. *The Tomb of Christ.* Phoenix Mill: Sutton, 1999.

Clapham, A.W. *The Latin Monastic Buildings of the Church of the Holy Sepulchre, Jerusalem.* Antiquaries Journal 1:3-18, 1921.

Conant, K.J. *Original Buildings at the Holy Sepulchre in Jerusalem.* Speculum 31:1-48, 1956.

Corbo, V.C. *Il Santo Sepolcro di Gerusalemme.* 3 vols. Jerusalem: Publications of the Studium Biblicum Franciscanum 29, 1981.

Coüasnon, C. *The Church of the Holy Sepulchre in Jerusalem.* London: Schweich Lectures of the British Academy, 1972 and 1974.

Folda, J. *The Art of the Crusaders in the Holy Land 1098-1187.* Cambridge: Cambridge University Press, 1995.

Gibson, S. and Taylor, J. *Beneath the Church of the Holy Sepulchre. The Archaeology and Early History of the Traditional Golgotha.* London: PEF Monograph 2, 1994.

Harvey, W. *Church of the Holy Sepulchre, Jerusalem. Structural Survey.* Oxford, 1935.

Hunt, E.D. *Holy Land Pilgrimage in the Later Roman Empire A.D. 312-460.* Oxford, 1984.

Jeffre, G. *A Brief Description of the Holy Sepulchre, Jerusalem, and other Christian Buildings in the Holy City.* Cambridge, 1919.

Peters, F.E. *Jerusalem: The Holy City in the Eyes of Chroniclers, Visitors, Pilgrims and Prophets from the Days of Abraham to the Beginnings of Modern Times.* Princeton: Princeton University Press, 1985.

Rock, A. *The Status Quo in the Holy Places.* Jerusalem: Holy Land Publications, 1989.

Rosovsky, N. (ed.). *City of the Great King: Jerusalem from King David to the Present.* Cambridge: Mass. and London, 1996.

Vincent, L. H. and Abel, F. M. *Jérusalem: Recherches de topographie, d'archéologie et d'histoire II, Jérusalem nouvelle,* fasc. I and II. Paris, 1914-26.

Wilkinson, J. *Jerusalem as Jesus Knew it: Archaeology as Evidence.* London, 1978.

Acknowledgments

It is our pleasant duty to thank all those who helped in the production of this book. Primarily we are thankful to the Church communities who granted our request to enter their home, the Church of the Holy Sepulchre, and record the people, the events and the physical surroundings that constitute the world that is the Holy Sepulchre. Thus we express our gratitude to: His Beatitude Diodorus I, the Greek Orthodox Patriarch of Jerusalem; His Beatitude Archbishop Torkum Manoogian, Armenian Patriarch of Jerusalem; The Most Reverend Father, Giovanni Battistelli, OFM, Custos of the Holy Land; His Eminence Archbishop Dr. Anba Abraham, Coptic Orthodox Metropolitan of Jerusalem and the Near East; His Eminence Mar Swerios Malki Murad, Syrian Orthodox Metropolitan and Patriarchal Vicar of Jerusalem, Jordan and the Holy Land and His Eminence Archbishop Matthewos, Head of the Ethiopian Orthodox Church in Jerusalem. We would also like to thank a number of individuals who provided specific assistance during our work: His Eminence Timothy, Senior Metropolitan of Vostra and Secretary General of the Greek Orthodox Patriarchate of Jerusalem; His Eminence Christodoulos, Metropolitan of Eleftheropolis and Chief Dragoman; His Eminence Daniel, Metropolitan of Tabor and Superior of the Church of the Holy Sepulchre; The Reverend Father Emilio Barcena, OFM; The Reverend Father Athanasius Macora, OFM; The Reverend Father Angelo, OFM; His Eminence Bishop Gureqh, Armenian Superior of the Holy Sepulchre; The Very Reverend Father Nourhan Manugian, Grand Sacristan of the Armenian Patriarchate, The Very Reverend Father Abedis, Dragoman of the Armenian Patriarchate; Vera and Anna Triandafillidou of the Russian Orthodox Palestine Society.

Additional invaluable support was provided by Amir Drori, director of the Israel Antiquities Authority, Jacob Fisch and other members of staff, who seized the opportunity and made this book possible. Further assistance in the field was given by Amit Reem of the IAA; Raanan Tal and Saliba Saliba from the Israel Police; Samir Farwagi of the Gloria Hotel; Kären Anderson de Zabé and Humberto Tachiquin who worked as photographic assistants to Michel Zabé; Birthe Kjølbye-Biddle who offered useful comments on the manuscript.

To all these individuals and to others whose names may have been inadvertently omitted we wish to express our gratitude and appreciation.

Credits

Printed in Italy